CROWN, COLLEGE AND RAILWAYS

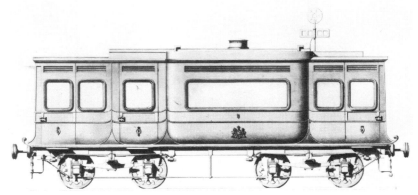

ABOVE: The 'North Star' was one of the most famous of the locomotives which operated on the Great Western main line. Built by Robert Stephenson and Co, it made the first run from Paddington to Maidenhead in 1838. The illustration shows the locomotive as re-built in 1854. (BR) BELOW: The Queen's Carriage 1848. A small disc-and-crossbar signal was provided on the roof to convey instructions to the footplate. (BR)

The Railway comes to Royal Windsor. This splendid print showing the South Western line crossing the Park on its way into Windsor, comes, curiously, from the Official Illustrated Guide to the Great Western Railway, 1860

A Barracuda Midnight Special

CROWN, COLLEGE AND RAILWAYS

HOW THE RAILWAYS CAME TO WINDSOR

BY

RAYMOND SOUTH

BARRACUDA BOOKS LIMITED
BUCKINGHAM, BUCKINGHAMSHIRE, ENGLAND
MCMLXXVIII

PUBLISHED BY BARRACUDA BOOKS LIMITED
BUCKINGHAM, ENGLAND
AND PRINTED BY
FRANK ROOK LIMITED
TOWER BRIDGE ROAD
LONDON SE1

BOUND BY
BOOKBINDERS OF LONDON LIMITED
LONDON N5

JACKET PRINTED BY
WHITE CRESCENT PRESS LIMITED
LUTON, ENGLAND

LITHOGRAPHY BY
SOUTH MIDLANDS LITHOPLATES LIMITED
LUTON, ENGLAND

DISPLAY TYPE SET IN
TIMES ROMAN SERIES 327
BY SOUTH BUCKS TYPESETTERS LIMITED
BEACONSFIELD, ENGLAND

TEXT SET IN 11pt PRESS ROMAN
BY BEAVER REPROGRAPHICS LIMITED
BUSHEY, ENGLAND

© Ray South 1978

ISBN 0 86023 071 6

CONTENTS

ACKNOWLEDGEMENTS

My research has taken me to many Record Offices and Libraries — notably the Royal Library at Windsor, Eton College, the House of Lords Record Office, the Public Record Office, the Berkshire County Record Office, the Reading Central Reference Library, the Windsor Guildhall and, last but not least, the *Windsor Express*, whose columns give a meticulous and often spirited local commentary on the story from beginning to end. Everywhere I have received encouragement and help, for which I am deeply grateful.

Acknowledgement is made in particular to the gracious permission of Her Majesty the Queen for the use made of the material from the Royal Archives and to the Provost and Fellows of Eton for access to the College Records.

Gordon Cullingham has again placed me under a debt of obligation for tracking down illustrations and helping over the maps which I hope will especially help those readers who do not know Windsor. Judith Hunter, Joe and Ruth Newman are among the others who have read the script and given me much practical help and advice. To Clive Birch of Barracuda I owe the opportunity to publish this story of a remarkable episode in railway history.

DEDICATION
To John Newman

FOREWORD

By Lt. Colonel the Lord Charteris of Amisfield, GCB GCVO OBE QSO

As the aeroplanes out of Heathrow snarl and thunder over Windsor Castle and Eton, they are in marked contrast to the locomotives, the soothing clatter of whose wheels helps to retain something of the rural atmosphere of these parts so it is not easy to comprehend why, 150 years or so ago Crown and College resisted with so much resolution the coming of the railways. Nor is it easy, at least for those who live and work at Eton, to appreciate how much power and influence the College had in those days.

All this and much else will be illuminated for those who read Mr. South's most interesting book. In his treatment of the Provost and Fellows he shows understanding of the difficulties which must have faced a body of elderly and middle aged clergymen in coming to terms with the invention of the steam locomotive. The College, in all but name a Dean and Chapter, had also to be mindful of their responsibilities as landlords; and more subtly, of the tacit opinions of their neighbours at the Castle, the descendants of the Founder. Mr. South shows very fairly how the College's attitude towards the irrevocable arrival of the railways at Windsor came to change. His criticism of the masters in sharper, and with reason. It must be remembered that they were concerned with discipline and obsessed with the fear that the railways would enable Etonians to get up to London and back within their hours of liberty. Today's increased hours of formal lessons, organised games, and cash limits, seem to preclude similar fears of New York and back by Concorde: but you can never tell!

Mr. South has earned the gratitude of the College archivist and of future students during his work on the records at Eton: his special knowledge enabled him to make a detailed list of the documents dealing with the railways. It is a pleasure for me to add my thanks, on behalf of the College, to Mr. South for that task; and to commend his description of a complicated and often delicate episode in the history of Windsor — and of Eton.

Charteris of Amisfield

9

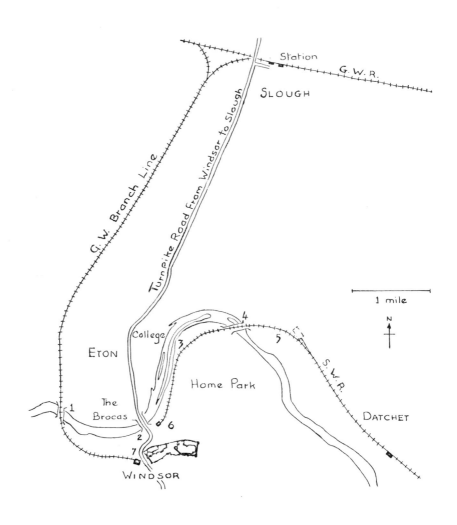

The Railways come to Windsor. The final pattern. Key: 1.
Brunel's Bridge 2. Windsor Bridge 3. Romney Island
4. Black Potts Bridge 5. Temporary Station-Black Potts
6. SW Station 7. GW Station

10

INTRODUCTION

The impact of the railways on nineteenth century England was revolutionary. Within twenty-five years of opening of the Stockton to Darlington Railway in 1825 a network of railways covered the country, linking London with the cities and towns of the provinces and with the seaports that were the gateways to the world beyond. The roads, the rivers, the more recent canals all fought a losing battle against the new form of communication and transport. The railways came to have almost every advantage over their rivals.

The importance of the railways to the industrial areas is obvious. But how did they affect towns like Windsor? In the 1830s Windsor was a small market town, distinguished from others only by the Castle and the presence of the Court. Between 1824 and 1836 the Castle was largely re-built and became the chief royal residence in the country. Queen Victoria and Prince Albert often spent the greater part of each year there, so that Windsor became one of the focal points in the life of the nation.

That this new status should be expressed in the construction of railways to serve the royal town seemed to many desirable and inevitable. But not to the Crown. For year after year the Crown authorities imposed a veto on every local railway project. Across the river Eton College was, if anything, even more implacable in its opposition to the coming of the railways. It would be an over-simplification to represent the confrontation between Crown and College on the one hand and the railway companies on the other as a conflict between old and new, between conservatism and progress. But both Court and College had their roots in the past; they needed time to adjust themselves to the forces of change which were sweeping the country. And the railways symbolised the new age of material progress and social change.

It was in 1833 that the first specific proposals to bring a

railway to Windsor were made. Fifteen years of frustration followed before Crown and College finally gave way and it was not until 1849 that the railways — not just one, but both the Great Western and the South Western — reached Windsor.

These fifteen years witnessed some of the most bitter conflicts in railway history. They saw the feud between the two great railway companies, the battle of the gauges, the short-lived experiment in atmospheric railways. They are the setting for the story of how two of the most powerful institutions in the country eventually accepted the railways after years of apparently uncompromising resistance.

Many of the important public figures of the mid-nineteenth century have prominent parts in the story: Peel, Gladstone and Disraeli among politicians; Russell, Chaplin and Saunders among railway administrators; Brunel, Robert Stephenson, Locke, Vignoles, Joseph Samuda among engineers; Eton headmasters Keate and Hawtrey; the Earl of Lincoln and Viscount Morpeth, Chief Crown Commissioners; the civic leaders of Windsor, of whom one at least — James Bedborough — was a man of outstanding ability and vision, and in the background — necessarily because of their position — the Queen and Prince Albert.

'The railways ousted the coaches with their smart equipages.' Coaches on the London to Reading Road near Slough, with the Castle (before its reconstruction) in the background. (RM)

FRUSTRATION

Windsor was deeply interested in all the projects to link London and Bristol by rail. These projects began in 1824-1825. Bristol merchants took the initiative in calling meetings and McAdam, the engineer, produced alternative plans for suitable routes. One of these proposed a route from Bristol to Wallingford by way of the Vale of the White Horse and thence along the right bank of the Thames by Reading, Wargrave and Bray to Brentford. These plans came to nothing and the same was true about other proposals. Perhaps in the circumstances of the time they were premature. The Stockton to Darlington Railway had indeed come into being in 1825, but was both remote and on a small scale. A railway from Bristol to London was a much more pretentious project and, until railways had proved themselves, was hardly likely to attract the necessary measure of support.

The success of the Liverpool to Manchester railway, opened in 1830, justified further attempts. Proposals for railways from London to Bristol, London to Southampton, London to Birmingham were embodied in parliamentary bills and all eventually — though not without many delays and frustrations — came to fruition. In 1832 two engineers, William Brunton and Henry Habberley Price, produced a circular headed *The Bristol and London Railway,* in which they proposed a route by Bath, Trowbridge and through the Vale of Pewsey to Hungerford, Newbury, Reading, Datchet, Colnbrook and Southall to Paddington. This again suggests a route through or near Windsor. The expense of the railway was estimated at £2,500,000 but even the promise of an interest of 15% was not sufficient to raise the money and the scheme was dropped at the beginning of 1833.

None the less Windsor had been given the hope that, when a railway linking Bristol and London was constructed — and to all who had faith in the future of the new means of communication this could only be a matter of time — it would pass through the royal town, its importance now enhanced by the reconstruction of the Castle and its use as the chief Royal residence. The immediate origins of the Great Western Railway Company belong to January 1833, when a number of Bristol merchants formed a committee to promote a railway. In May I.K. Brunel, already renowned in Bristol as the designer of the projected Clifton suspension bridge, was appointed as engineer. He was then only 27 and had before him a distinguished career in the development of the country's railways, particularly those of the Great Western. Very soon, a second key appointment was made when Charles Alexander Saunders became Secretary of the new Railway Company. He was to play an influential part in the development of the Great Western railway system, a part complementary to and hardly less important than that of Brunel himself. Certainly more than Brunel, he was deeply involved in the diplomacy of the protracted negotiations with the Crown and with Eton College which preceded the agreements which, sixteen years later, brought the Great Western to Windsor.

Brunel's preliminary plans did not exclude the possibility of the railway passing through Windsor. The *Windsor Express* reported: 'The Great Western Railway between Bristol and London . . . is to have a double-line as far as Maidenhead, passing direct in one, and by Kingston, Staines and Windsor in the other'. However, by the time the plans were finally deposited in November 1833, the route by way of Slough had been adopted, with a branch line to Windsor.

This evoked anger and dismay in Windsor. The *Express* commented: 'If the Union of Bristol and London be an object of such national importance, how can that object be more directly and effectually promoted than by a Railroad through Windsor?'. All the evidence goes to show that Windsor's leading citizens were fully sensible of the importance of the railway to the town. James Bedborough was always in the forefront, as he was until success was finally achieved in 1849, but he received staunch support from his colleagues on the Council. The Maidenhead Council, on the other hand, was extremely apprehensive about the coming of the railways. A letter from Charles Saunders, asking for the consent and encouragement of the Corporation, met with a cool response. The main fear of the Corporation was that the railway would adversely affect the revenue derived from the bridge tolls — as many as 60 or

80 coaches alone passed daily along the Bath Road and through the town – and, without a legal undertaking from the Railway Company about compensation, opposition to the Great Western Bill was maintained. As late as June 1834 the Corporation resolved 'that the opposition to the progress of the Bill shall be continued up to the latest moment'.

In the meantime the Great Western went ahead with its Bill. An early casualty was the Slough to Windsor Branch. Windsor might have reconciled itself to the branch line when it became clear that there was no hope of achieving a main line status. The opposition of Eton College, however, was decisive. Already, immediately following the publication of the Great Western plans for the railway, the Provost, Dr. Goodall, had made it clear at a meeting held at Salt Hill, Slough, that 'the College would endeavour to prevent it to the utmost of their abilities and the extent of their purse'. At a meeting at the Windsor Guildhall on 10 January 1834 Dr. Keate, now in his last year as Eton's headmaster, said 'it will be impossible to keep the boys from this railroad in their hours of liberty . . . I cannot help thinking that it will very materially endanger the discipline of the School'. In reference to Keate's remarks, John Secker, Windsor's Town Clerk and himself an Old Etonian, commented: 'you have been told that one of the great objections to the construction of a railroad in the neighbourhood of Eton is that the young gentlemen of the College will be mischievously inclined and that they will do that which will occasion great danger to the passengers'. To which Keate replied: 'not wilfully or intentionally, but in playfulness'.

In the light of the disinclination of the Great Western Company to favour a line passing through Windsor, local support was given to 'The London and Windsor Railway Company'. References to this new project first appeared in the *Express* in September 1833 and were soon followed by official notices in October and a detailed prospectus in November. An influential Committee was formed which included both of Windsor's MPs, John Ramsbottom and Sir Samuel Pechell, as well as the Mayor, Robert Blunt, and the Town Clerk, John Secker. Several possible routes were suggested at different times, crossing the Park both to the south and the north of the Castle. First proposals were 'to approach the town on the Frogmore side, crossing the Thames by a bridge at Southley', but by November the proposed route had been changed to approach Windsor from Colnbrook 'across the River Thames and . . . . enter Windsor by a Terrace to be erected on the North-side of the Home Park'. The Eton College Records contain copies of a plan showing this latter route, crossing the Thames and then continuing near the south side of the river to a terminus in the neighbourhood of Clewer. This would leave open the possibility of an extension to Reading.

The promoters were fully aware that 'one obstacle appeared to present itself, namely — that this plan could not be effectual without crossing the Home Park, or the Crown's property without its walls'. An approach was made to the King, William IV, and His Majesty, according to the *Windsor Express* of 23 November 1833, 'graciously consented to sanction any arrangement that might be made with the Office of Woods . . . in order that it might enter the town by Datchet-lane, cross Thames Street and terminate at the back of the town'. The enemies of the project were quick to show scepticism. The *Berkshire Chronicle,* which was as vehement in its opposition as the *Windsor Express* was in support, commented, 'We certainly think that the name of an illustrious personage has been made use of by some of the promoters of the scheme in a manner — to say the least — totally unwarrantable'. The King's 'consent' was often quoted in later years when the approval of the Crown was sought. For instance, in August 1845, reference was made to 'the consent of his late Majesty for a Railway into Windsor'.

The question is, to what kind of a railway did the King give his consent? The *Express* said, 'The London and Windsor Railway Company propose to use horses instead of steam-coaches. The travelling is to be performed in carriages drawn by a single horse'. This was by no means impossible. Until 1836 — or later — some engineers still considered that stationary engines with cables *or horses* were preferable to locomotives. It does, however, raise a query whether the King's 'yes' in 1833 was a valid precedent in 1845.

The Windsor Corporation gave the London and Windsor Company its full support. A Petition to the House of Commons asking for leave to bring in a Bill was signed by an impressive array of Windsor's leading citizens. The extent of public interest in the town is evidenced by the Railway Meeting held at the Guildhall on 10 January 1834 and reported verbatim in the *Express* of the two following weeks. The report runs to thirteen columns and its length was justified by the Editor because of 'the overwhelming interest of this subject as connected with this town and neighbourhood'. Among the speakers was Charles Vignoles, the famous engineer who was later to be associated with the attempts to bring an atmospheric railway to Windsor. In the course of a lengthy and closely reasoned speech he argued that a line from London to Reading by way of Windsor would be infinitely preferable to one via Maidenhead. The sense of the meeting was expressed in a resolution proposed by John Secker and seconded by James Bedborough, that 'the proposed London and Windsor Railway will be of the utmost advantage and importance to the inhabitants of Windsor and the country adjacent whether viewed merely as a railway communicating from London to Windsor or ultimately as a portion of the best line between the metropolis and the West of England'.

The more ambitious view was in fact steadily gaining ground. The editor of the *Express* commented that the issue was not between 'railers' and 'anti-railers', but 'whether or not this town ought to be made a passing-place to the whole of the west of England'.

Support for the London and Windsor project came from a report prepared by Henry Habberley Price, the engineer who was involved in the surveying of possible routes between London and Bristol. The title of the report refers to 'a Grand Western Railway Communication from London into South Wales' (an interesting reference at this stage to the possible extension beyond Bristol), 'with a comparative view of the merits of the London and Reading and London and Windsor Railway scheme'. The report, dated 7 March 1834, was prepared for the Earl of Jersey, as the route of the London to Windsor railway was likely to pass through his property at Osterley Park. It examines the rival merits of the two proposals and quite unequivocally recommends the Windsor route as superior. Price recognises that the London and Windsor should, if constructed, 'be considered as the foundation for a Great Western Railway; inasmuch as it cannot for a moment be supposed that two railways parallel to each other, or nearly so, from Reading or Windsor to London, can be necessary or would be permitted by Parliament'. 'If,' however', he continues 'the Bristol scheme is persevered in before a parliamentary committee, it is perfectly evident the Windsor gentlemen have no other course left them to pursue than to withdraw their Bill this session, in full confidence that Parliament will not sanction the opposing measure'.

The Windsor Council was encouraged by Price's Report to go ahead with its Petition against the Great Western Bill. The latter, however, was making progress and on 10 March 1834 received its Second Reading in the House of Commons by 182 votes to 92. Not long after this, the promoters of the London and Windsor project — to the dismay of its supporters — withdrew their measure. This retreat may have been due at least as much to financial as to other difficulties. In the Eton College Records there are copies of a printed broadsheet entitled 'Windsor Railway. Practice versus Theory', dated 3 February 1834 and signed 'VERITAS'. It is primarily a critical and sometimes sarcastic commentary on the finances of the Company. The Bill was referred to a committee of which Lord Granville Somerset was chairman. (He had also moved the Second Reading.) The Committee first met on 16 April and, such was the opposition, continued until well into the summer.

Foremost among the enemies of the Bill were the authorities of Eton College which, as one correspondent to the *Berkshire Chronicle* put it, 'has been, and still is and, I hope, will ever be the fostering mother of almost all the aristocracy of wealth and birth that proud England can boast of'. What was perhaps more to the point, the College certainly had a large representation in Parliament and, although the Bill survived the long ordeal before the Commons Committee and went on to pass through the House of Commons by a small majority, in the Lords it was defeated by 47 votes to 30. The Old Etonian peers had won the day for the College.

Hardly had the rejoicing of the Bill's opponents subsided, however, before the Great Western launched a second — and this time successful — attempt. A prospectus was issued in September 1834 and in the following month a public meeting, held at Merchants' Hall, Bristol, was attended (*inter alia*) by representatives from Windsor — still hoping no doubt to win support for a route that would pass through the town. Charles Stuart Voules, a Windsor solicitor, pressed the case for what he called 'a slight deviation from their original line, so as to take in the town of Windsor. They might tunnel under the Long Walk and so pass by Windsor Castle without being either seen or heard'. This envisaged a route across the Park to the *south* of the Castle, which helps to explain why Voules could go on to state that 'the Provost of Eton had declared to him, that he did not perceive that any mischief would arise from the line that he proposed, and consequently would not offer any opposition'. Sir Samuel Pechell MP, who had been elected for Windsor in the preceding year as a Court candidate, went even further and said that 'his Majesty knew of his purpose of attending the meeting and, moreover, that he had the sanction of the Commissioners of Woods and Forests to affirm that it met with their support'. This was certainly a bold attempt to convince the Bristol meeting that a route through Windsor could gain the support of both Crown and College. Charles Saunders was however, unconvinced and much later, in 1846, James Bedborough recalled how Saunders in the course of a long speech had asked: 'what good would it be to have a railway through Windsor and pass such an important town as Maidenhead?'

There was a suspicion of sarcasm in Saunders' comment which was hardly likely to placate Windsor. It was unfortunate that the passage of the second Great Western Bill through Parliament coincided with the Municipal Reform Bill which, for Windsor as for many other towns, spelt the end of an era. No Council meeting was held from December 1834 to September 1835. If there was to be an organised and effective opposition to the Bill, this was the vital period, but the Windsor Council seems to have given up the ghost. By the time the newly elected Council held its first meeting on 31 December 1835, the Great Western Bill had been on the statute book for several months. Among the early records of the new Council is the decision, in June 1836, to sell fifteen perches of land at Langley for the purpose of the railway. Only two years before, in February 1834, a similar application to purchase the land had met with a resolute refusal from the Windsor Corporation. The Maidenhead Council, on the other hand, having received reassurances on the possible loss of revenue from the bridge tolls, now gave strong support to the Bill. At a meeting held in February 1835 the Council agreed to forward Petitions in its favour both to the House of Commons and to the House of Lords and recorded its opinion that the Bill was 'calculated in an eminent degree to benefit the Town of Maidenhead'.

In the circumstances, therefore, the local opposition to the railway depended largely on Eton College. Eton's opposition to the second Great Western Bill is in fact better documented than in the case of the first Bill, since more of the parliamentary records have survived. The pattern of Eton's opposition, however, never varied; what was said in 1835 was the same as what had been said in 1833 and 1834 and indeed — at least so far as the Masters and many Old Etonians were concerned — the same as in 1848.

Eton's opposition to the railway is prominent in the College Records of the time. First and foremost is the evidence given to the House of Lords Select Committee on 11 August 1835. At Westminster this forms a minute part of the large printed volume which contains the evidence given in the summer of 1835. The College, however, had its own evidence extracted and printed separately in booklets, several copies of which survive in the Records.

Dr. Keate had gone by this time and his successor as headmaster, Dr. Edward Hawtrey, who was in later years to be a formidable and unyielding antagonist of the railway, does not appear at this enquiry. The burden of presenting the Eton case fell upon Rev. Thomas Carter, Fellow and Bursar of the College, and Rev. William Gifford Cookesley, one of the masters. Carter, who had a secondary interest in the route of the railway as Vicar of Burnham, said that Eton was totally opposed to the railway. The 'Feeling of Opposition . . . has never altered; it is as strong as at the very first'.

The following dialogue then ensued: 'Is there any objection to the facilities afforded to the ready passage of the boys to this town [i.e. London]?'

'That was the great objection and a very strong one'.

'Did the objection arise also from the facilities afforded to the constant access of visitors from town?'

'I suppose it would have given access frequently; wherever the depot was we should always be subject to cabs and omnibuses which would lead to much greater facility of communication'.

'Is there any objection then to the institution of such a railway as this in such a direction, with reference to it, practically speaking, shortening the distance between Eton and London?'

'Yes; we conceive it would give the boys the facility between every school time of running up to London and back again in the hours they have to themselves'.

'Is there any other feeling with reference to any practical danger from the railway?'

'It would be impossible to keep the boys from the railway; anybody who knows the nature of boys, or Eton Boys, will fully agree in that.'

Carter went on to say that the provision of a wall or the use of police would be ineffective. Asked whether the College had been prepared to agree to a line to the south of the Castle, Carter replied that 'it was only less objectionable as being more difficult of access to the boys'. The dialogue continued: 'You think the Railway passing any way nearer to Eton than four miles would be detrimental to the school?'

'Yes'.

'Do you think they could not restrain the boys going five miles from Eton to a railroad?'

'No; a horse is such a quick mode; and they have their time. A master may catch them up; but it is not known how they are employed.'

When the Rev. William Gifford Cookesley followed, he had to face the point that Harrow did not object to the Birmingham Railway; why should Eton oppose the Great Western? Cookesley replied that he did not think that the case of Eton was comparable to that of other schools because 'the tone and habit, and more especially the wealth and rank of the boys at Eton must be taken into the account. They had not been able to pass sumptuary laws to prevent boys having more money than does them good'.

The system at Eton, continued Cookesley, depends on 'giving the boys as much freedom as is consistent with discipline'. The proximity of a railway would undermine this principle. The great principle of the school was letting the boys go where they like and when they like, conformable with the discipline of the school. 'If', he said, 'the parent of a boy at Eton was to come and say, you did not take decent precautions to prevent my boy coming upon the railway and getting into vice, we should feel we had neglected that boy.'

Carter, recalled on 13 August, said in answer to a question that the last meeting at the College concerning the railroad was at the beginning of June. Saunders, who was present, was told that the College 'would do everything that lay within their power to stop the progress of the railway'.

Eton's opposition was not completely negative. They had an alternative suggestion which had the merit of by-passing the College at a distance of some fifteen miles — a distance which even the College authorities might consider to be 'safe'. The proposal is outlined in an attractively printed broadsheet entitled *Eton College Case* and reads: 'It having been discovered within these few days that a Western Railway can be made not only by way of Basing, but also by preserving the plan of the Great Western Railway Company as between Bristol and Reading; and then diverting the line into the valley of the Blackwater River, joining the Southampton line at Farnborough, . . . making a difference in distance of only 6 or 7 miles, which in point of time according to the evidence as to the rate of speed will not exceed a quarter of an hour, — thereby avoiding the necessity of cutting up any part of the counties of Middlesex, & Bucks, or of interfering with the River Thames at Maidenhead, and bringing the railway so near to the College of Eton, that it cannot fail to endanger the safety of the scholars, cause repeated breaches to be made in the discipline of the school, and subject the College to the constant apprehension of an application for a branch from this line to Windsor; the consequence of which would be fatal to the prosperity of Eton. The Provost and Fellows therefore feel bound as the Guardians of their Establishment to show that as this latter line can be easily attained, the present proposed one ought not to receive the sanction of Parliament'.

The statement was accompanied by a plan and so continued: 'It will be at once seen by the sketch that a saving can be made of the enormous sums which will be required to purchase lands and compensate parties on the line from London to Reading, as the line from the latter place to Farnborough will pass through Waste or Forest Land, or Lands of comparatively little value, & without entrenching on private residences.

Under these circumstances, therefore, it is to be hoped that every Friend to the Establishment of Eton College will give them such support as will cause the present line to be abandoned.'

The appeal in the final paragraph of the statement to 'every Friend to the Establishment of Eton College' more than hints at the other weapon which, as we have seen already, was always available — the presence in both Houses of Parliament of a considerable number of Old Etonians.

When the Great Western Bill was before the House of Lords Select Committee, Thomas Batcheldor, the College Registrar, wrote to inform the Duke of Newcastle about the course of the proceedings: 'I am instructed to continue the opposition on the part of the College and to make known their anxious desire to get rid of the Bill'. When the Bill was coming up for its final reading in the Lords — and in the previous year 47 peers had been sufficient to defeat the Great Western — a letter signed (*inter alia*) by Goodall, Carter, Coleridge and Cookesley, was sent to all peers. It began: 'pray oblige us by perusing and supporting personally and by your interest the following case'. (This is almost certainly a reference to the 'Eton College Case' described above.) 'The best interests of Eton are involved in the rejection of the Great Western Railroad Bill.' The letter includes a special appeal to Old Etonians — 'more especially from those who have personally experienced in their youth the benefit of the system of Eton School'. The King's brother, the Duke of Cumberland, spoke in the Second Reading debate in the Lords and referred to 'the injurious effect' which the measure 'was likely to have upon the great seminary in which their Lordships must feel so strong an interest'. It was said that Etonian peers attended and voted who had never been seen in the precincts of Westminster.

None the less this time the College was unsuccessful in its opposition and the Bill eventually received the Royal Assent on 31 August 1835. However, if the College had not been able to prevent the final passing of the Bill, its opposition had been decisive where the branch line with Windsor was concerned and it was able to insist on the insertion in the Bill of a formidable series of safeguards. Chief among these was the prohibition of any station or future railway within three miles of the College.

Windsor had secured nothing. It had seen its own favoured bill jettisoned, and it had failed completely to persuade the Great Western to bring its main line through Windsor. It had not even secured the modest consolation of a branch line from Slough — for this it had to wait another fourteen years. From time to time the branch line project was revived, but the high hopes of 1833 — 1834 had faded and Windsor seemed resigned to its defeat.

One immediate effect of the clauses inserted in the 1835 Act to safeguard the interests of Eton was to prevent the Company from building a station at Slough. More than two years elapsed after the passing of the Act before the matter became urgent. Then, in the early months of 1838, as the time approached for the opening of the first section of the main line from Paddington to Taplow, the pressure on the College to agree to a station at Slough increased. The College, however, remained obdurate. Memorials signed by the Mayor of Windsor,

William Bonsey of Slough and other local citizens brought this reply: 'The Provost and College of Eton, having carefully weighed the contents of the Memorials presented to them with regard to the proposed establishment of a station on the Great Western Rail Road at Slough, feel regret in stating to the Memorialists that they consider it their paramount duty in support of the interests of the College and school to withhold their consent to such application and to claim the protection granted to them by the clauses contained in the Act of Parliament.' Simultaneously, approaches were also made to the Great Western, and on 20 April 1838 Charles Saunders wrote to William Bonsey, a local solicitor who was the chief spokesman for Slough: 'They the directors will deem it their duty to stop certain trains as they pass through Slough, for the purpose of allowing travellers to alight from their carriages, or to join them; and they will take the best means of preserving order and regularity at the point where the trains will be stopped, so far as can be done consistently with the injunction of the legislature.'

This was not the first intimation of the intention of the Company, and the College now applied to the Court of Chancery for an injunction to stop such an evasion of the spirit of the Act. The opening of the railway was due to take place on 4 June and, two days before, Eton's application had been dismissed with costs. An appeal followed, but the Lord Chancellor upheld the decision of the Court of Chancery, ruling that the directors of the Company were entitled to do anything not expressly forbidden by the Act.

Strangely, even while the appeal was pending, the College asked the Company to provide a special train to take the boys up to town for the Coronation on 28 June and this was done.

From 4 June — Whit Monday and the day of the Eton Regatta — a regular train service was maintained. For two years passengers who boarded trains at Slough — including those from Windsor who were still denied their own line and their own station — had until September 1838 to book at the Crown Inn and thereafter at 'the New House in Stoke Lane'.

Neither the Great Western Company nor Windsor was prepared to leave matters in this unsatisfactory state. A letter from the Company, as early as 9 July 1838, said that if the College agreed to a station 'the Company will engage to appoint and maintain in the said station two persons to be selected by the

Provost or headmaster, for the purpose of preventing any Eton boys passing to the railway without the sanction of any of the masters'. Batcheldor's reply on behalf of the College said that, whatever the Vice-Chancellor's ruling was, the intention of the Committee of the House of Lords with regard to the station was clear and the GWR had committed 'a breach of Faith towards the College'. If they wanted further discussion, they ought first by some public act to 'set themselves right with the College'. Another letter, dated 6 August 1838, from the Company, over the signature of William Sims, a director, declined to give way on the matter of trains stopping at Slough. He repeated that his 'brother directors are desirous of meeting the views of the College authorities in any manner calculated to conciliate them or to secure the interests of the institution', but wished to press the desire for a station. In a postscript he added, 'My own opinion is that the regulations which can be enforced at a station must tend very materially to the security and advantage of the College in all points that affect the discipline of the school'. Meetings did in fact take place between the Company and the College both on 19 July and 28 November 1838. On the latter occasion, 'the Windsor people attended; but the appeals met with no immediate response.

Prince Albert made his first journey by train — from Slough to Paddington — on 14 November 1839. After his marriage to Queen Victoria three months later, he used the Great Western regularly and, although it was another two years before the Queen herself travelled by train, there was the hope of royal patronage in the not too distant future. By 1840 the first Royal Saloon had been built — a sumptuous affair 'fitted up with crimson and white silk and exquisitely executed paintings representing the four elements'. But for a time at least all this was still in the future, and the Prince and any other noteable visitor to the Castle who chose to use the railway had to mount the train at Slough without the convenience of a station.

Whether this influenced the College there appears to be no evidence to show, but certainly Eton's attitude changed in 1839. Among the College Records are several papers which suggest that the College was now prepared to agree to a station at Slough and also to a Windsor to Slough branch line subject to adequate safeguards. There is the draft of an Agreement between the College and the 'Windsor and Slough Railway

Company' 'previous to Application for the Bill'. It bears the name of T. Batcheldor and contains many of the future safeguards such as fencing, police, no station at Eton. This is followed by a full agreement between the Provost and Fellows of Eton College and W. Chadwick, agent for the intended Windsor and Slough Railway Company. The agreement includes the phrase, 'Whereas the said Railway Company are about establishing a railway from Slough to Windsor in connexion with the Great Western Railway'. Nothing came, however, of the branch line project – James Bedborough said of the Bill at a parliamentary enquiry in 1847 'it did not go into Parliament'. Perhaps this time it was the Crown rather than the College which scotched it. The Company was none the less able to go ahead with the building of the station. A letter from the Great Western Solicitors to the Provost gave notice of 'an application to repeal and amend as much of the 1835 Act as is necessary to provide for a station at Slough'. Thomas Batcheldor informed the Chairman of the Company that 'The College Authorities, although they have an insuperable objection to affixing their corporate seal to the consent required, will take no step in opposition', and the station was opened in June 1840, and until the construction of the Windsor Branch nine years later was known as the Slough and Windsor station. By this time the main line was open as far as Steventon and, almost exactly a year later, in June 1841, the whole line was open from London through to Bristol.

OPPOSITE: Notice of the London and Windsor Railway Company 1833– the first local railway project. (WE)

LONDON & WINDSOR RAILWAY COMPANY.

To be incorporated by Act of Parliament.

Capital £300,000.

In 10,000 Shares, of £30 each, Deposit £1 per Share.

LONDON COMMITTEE.	WINDSOR COMMITTEE.
A. H. Holdsworth, Esq.	John Ramsbottom, Esq. M.P.
George Thackrah, Esq.	Sir Samuel Brook Pechell, M.P.
William Hamilton, Esq.	R. Blunt, Esq. Mayor.
John Farnell, Esq.	C. Snowden, Esq. Justice.
Charles Perkins, Esq.	John Secker, Esq. Town Clerk.
Henry Hunt, Esq.	
John Kirkland, Esq.	
Augustus Applegath, Esq.	
William Ellward, jun. Esq.	

BANKERS.

Messrs. Curries and Co. London.	Messrs. Ramsbottom and Legh, Windsor.

SOLICITORS.

Messrs. Karslake and Crealock, No. 4, Carlton Chambers, Regent Street.

SECRETARY.

R. S. Young, Esq. No. 7, Tokenhouse Yard.

ENGINEER.

Joseph Gibbs, Esq., Architect.

SURVEYORS.

Messrs. Cruckshank and Gilbert, Furnival's Inn.

Applications for Shares to be made by letter to the Secretary, or Solicitors.

The detailed prospectus and plan will be shortly published.

LONDON and WINDSOR RAILWAY. Notice is hereby given, that application is intended to be made to Parliament in the next Session, for an Act to make and maintain a Railway, or Railways, Branch Railway, or Railways, with proper warehouses, wharfs, landing places, bridges, and other works, and conveniences adjoining thereto, or connected therewith, commencing on the west side of the high road, called the Edgeware Road, leading from London to Edgeware, at or near to the works of the Grand Junction Water Company, in the parish of Paddington, in the county of Middlesex, and terminating at or near to Clewer Field, or Clewer Meadow, in the parish of Clewer, on the western side of the town of Windsor, in the county of Berks; and which said Railway or Railways is or are intended to pass into or through the several parishes, townships, or places of Paddington, Bayswater, Westbourn Green, Kensington, Kensington Gravel Pits, Fulham, Shepherds Bush, Hammersmith, North Highway, Starch Green, East Acton, Acton, Chiswick, Gunnersbury, Ealing Common, Ealing, Little Ealing, Brentford, Hanwell, Hanwell Heath, Osterley, Norwood, Southall, Heston, North Hyde, Hayes, Cranford, Harlington, otherwise Arlington, Binckwell, Sipson, West Drayton, Harmondsworth, Stanwell, and Colnbrook, or some of them, all in the county of Middlesex. Colnbrook, Iver, Langley, otherwise Langley Marish, Horton, Ditton Green, Datchet, Southley, Upton, otherwise Upton-cum-Chalvey, and Eton, or some of them, all in the county of Buckingham. New Windsor, Windmill Field, Clewer, Clewer Field, or Clewer Meadow, or some of them, all in the county of Berks.

Dated the 9th day of October, 1833.

KARSLAKE & CREALOCK, Solicitors,
4, Regent Street, Waterloo Place, London.

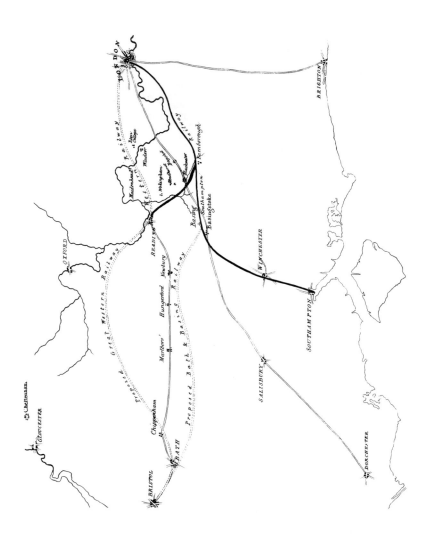

Plan of Eton College proposal for an alternative route for the Great Western main line 1835, which would have kept the railway well away from Eton

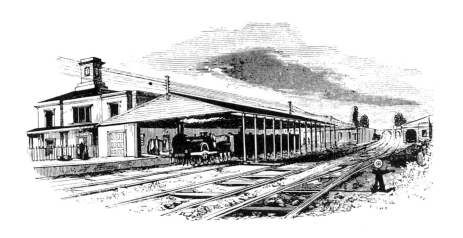

ABOVE: Slough Station. An early print from Masson's 'Guide to the Great Western Railway', 1852. The Station, opened in June 1840, consisted of two separate buildings, some distance apart, for Down and Up traffic respectively. BELOW: The North Star, one of the most famous of the locomotives which operated on the GW main line.

Contemporary print of a train at the Slough Station before the construction of the Windsor branch. The Royal Hotel is in the background; two reception rooms, luxuriously furnished, were reserved for the Queen's use. (GC)

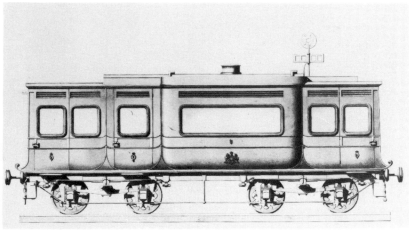

*ABOVE: Queen Victoria's first railway journey, from
Slough to Paddington, June 13, 1842. (ILN) BELOW:
The Queen's carriage 1848. (BR)*

31

Charles Saunders, Secretary and General Superintendent of the Great Western Railway, 1833-63. (BR)

NO NOISE OR SMOKE

By 1844 the framework of the English railway system was taking shape. From London it was possible to travel by way of Birmingham as far north-west as Lancaster, or even via Newcastle to Carlisle. Many of the northern industrial cities and ports were already linked with each other and with the Metropolis — not only Newcastle, but also Liverpool, Manchester, Leeds and Hull. The Eastern Counties had reached Cambridge and was stretching out towards Norwich and Yarmouth. To the south Dover, Brighton and Southampton were all linked by rail to London, while to the west the main Great Western line to Bristol had been continued by the Bristol and Exeter to the latter city.

Windsor, however, despite its increasing importance in the life of the nation since Queen Victoria and Prince Albert had made the Castle their principal place of residence, remained without a railway. James Bedborough told a House of Commons Select Committee in 1846, 'I think there is no town in the kingdom that is so badly off for the want of a railway, *having such wants as Windsor to be supplied with one'.*

For almost ten years the nearest the railway came to Windsor was two-and-a-half miles away at Slough. This became the normal route from Windsor to London, or vice-versa. The coaches which for many years had plied between Windsor and London were almost forced out of business. When Henry Thumwood, who had been the Windsor coach-master in the days before the coming of the railway, was asked in 1847: 'Did the establishing of the Great Western Railway interfere with your trade'?, his forthright reply was, 'It knocked it all up'.

John Whitehouse, toll-collector at the Slough Road Gate, gave details of the annual traffic between Slough and Windsor, based mainly upon a fourteen days' sample count in the first half of October 1845. The figures for individuals passing the toll-gate were given as: by omnibus: 140,785; post horses:

33

63,022; private vehicles and horses: 90,806; foot passengers: 353,998, giving a total of 648,611. In addition Ascot Race Week accounted for 35,000 over and above normal.

There were seventeen trains each way every day between Slough and Paddington and 'a constant stream of passengers' throughout the year. Sometimes the omnibuses could not take all those who wished to travel on from Slough to Windsor, and walking was the only alternative. At best the omnibuses were often overcrowded; the segregation into first, second and often third class passengers provided for on the trains did not apply to the omnibuses, with the result that 'ladies and soldiers' might have to sit together.

In the reverse direction Windsor residents complained not only about the time consumed in getting to Slough but also about the inconvenience of Paddington. John Secker, Windsor's Town Clerk, said, 'I am frequently more than two hours and a quarter getting into a working part of London – a business part of London'. It was in fact not only the time taken in getting by omnibus from Windsor to Slough, but the time consumed in waiting at Paddington – often passengers had to stay in the train until goods and luggage had been cleared – and then the time taken in getting across London by omnibus or cab that rankled. Plans to move the Great Western terminus 'into the heart of London' were too remote to assuage the dissatisfaction.

In both directions the traffic between Slough and Windsor had to pass through Eton, with 'the constant nuisance of cabs, omnibuses, driving through'. Then, as now, the College buildings were divided on either side of the main road, with boys frequently passing from one side to the other; and Eton High Street was a long narrow thoroughfare leading to Windsor Bridge. This state of affairs led to the obvious argument that a railway by-passing Eton would, amongst other benefits, remove much of the traffic that passed through the town. To this Dr. Hawtrey, the headmaster, replied, 'I should compare it to cutting off my leg instead of cutting off my little finger'.

It was against this background that the Windsor railway projects of 1844 and 1845 were launched. These were still pioneering days in railway development and the Windsor proposals were for *atmospheric* railways. The locomotive engine had not yet established itself finally against all competing forms of traction. Steam coaches, using the roads, had come and gone, but the trustworthy horse had not been completely discarded.

Stationary engines, especially for coping with gradients, still had their advocates. The atmospheric railways were an episode in this period of experiment. Whereas the horse and the stationary engine, however, were associated with the past and the colliery railways, atmospheric traction looked to the future.

We are inclined perhaps to view the early locomotives through rose-coloured spectacles. The harsh reality is that not only did they frequently break down, but they were noisy and dirty and the use of open carriages made smoke as well as rain an unpleasant accompaniment to travel. Hence the search for a more acceptable alternative to the steam locomotive — and for a brief period the atmospheric railway seemed to many the answer. First patented by Samuel Clegg and Jacob and Joseph Samuda in 1838, the system was rapidly developed. Trials were held at Wormwood Scrubbs in 1840, where Prince Albert himself went to see them. By 1843 sufficient progress had been made for the construction of the Kingstown to Dalkey atmospheric line at Dublin. The engineer for this was Charles Vignoles, who in 1845 became engineer for the Windsor, Slough and Staines Atmospheric Railway. He was one of a number of engineers who were attracted by the atmospheric system. Another — and the most famous — was Brunel. The first English prospectus of an atmospheric railway, in January 1844, was for the Gravesend, Rochester and Chatham Railway, with Brunel as engineer. This failed to receive parliamentary approval, but later in the same year plans were drawn up for the construction of a single-track atmospheric railway, 52 miles long, between Exeter and Plymouth. Brunel came near to staking his reputation on the short-lived experiment of the South Devon railway and he was largely responsible for the Exeter to Teignmouth section which was opened in September 1847.

Other engineers, like Robert Stephenson, were contemptuous of the project from the start and would have nothing to do with it. He was the most prominent of the contemporary sceptics but by no means the last. It became the fashion to decry the idea of atmospheric traction as 'a thoroughly unpractical system'. At the time, however, it seemed to many the hope of the future. Both Sir Robert Peel, the Prime Minister, and W.E. Gladstone, President of the Board of Trade, appreciated the possibilities of the atmospheric system and thought it should have a full trial.

In the atmospheric system a cast-iron tube was laid between

the rails, and the air inside the tube was removed by stationary engines placed at intervals along the track. Trains were pulled by a 'motor carriage' — a truck with a piston, which fitted closely inside the iron tube suspended beneath it.

At the top of the iron tube was a 2½in wide continuous slit which was covered by a leather flap attached to one side of it. The motor carriage truck included a device which would lift the leather flap, allowing air to enter the empty tube, and also a roller which would force the leather down on to the slit so that the air in the tube might be exhausted again. Propulsion occurred when air was admitted behind the piston causing the piston and hence the motor carriage truck to move towards the section of the tube which had no air in it.

Not only did the atmospheric system eliminate noise and smoke, but it could produce high speeds. When Prince Albert watched the trials on 29 June 1840, a speed of 40 mph was reached and at the trials preceding the opening of the Dublin Railway speeds of up to 60 mph were attained. Hence the confident assumption that the 25 mile journey from Windsor to London could be accomplished in half-an-hour.

The equable motion of the Atmospheric was another merit urged in its favour. The *Windsor Express* described a test carried out on the Croydon railway. 'The test was most simple and unerring. A halfpenny was placed on the step of the carriage, and though the train passed to and from the whole length of the atmospheric line (5 miles), yet not only was the coin not ejected from the step, but so uniform had the motion been that, on measuring the distance it had moved, half an inch was sufficient to cover it'.

On 12 October 1844 a notice appeared in the advertisement columns of the *Windsor Express:* 'The Proposed Windsor Junction Railway' is intended to connect the Station, near Windsor Bridge, with Staines, through Datchet, in one separate atmospheric line, so as to join the contemplated Staines and Richmond Junction Railway, and by it the Richmond and Hungerford Bridge line, thus forming one line from Windsor to the neighbourhood of Whitehall and Charing Cross.'

This was the first of many projects in 1844 and 1845, nearly all of which died an early death. Most proposed to use the atmospheric system; one notice indeed stated that 'the Atmospheric principle' would be used *'if deemed advisable'.* In the current flush of enthusiasm, however, few seemed to think even this modest reservation necessary. 'The Atmospheric principle', asserted the *Express,* is now declared by many eminent engineers to be most advantageous for short lines with frequent traffic, near large towns, where the absence of noise and smoke is important.'

The question, however, of the best route into Windsor was beset with doubts and difficulties. All were aware that the attitude of the Crown would be decisive, but a spirit of optimism prevailed. 'We cannot conceive', said the *Express,* 'that the project would be objected to by our most Gracious Sovereign, were it fairly presented to her notice.' The representatives of the Crown were certainly fully informed of proposals and developments, but for the time being they remained silent spectators. Proposals and plans proliferated. There were proposals for viaducts, embankments, bridges, cuttings — even a tunnel under the Long Walk. There were plans for routes by way of Frogmore to the south of the Castle, and on the line of the towpath to the north of the Castle. There were designs for terminal stations near the Bridge, or 'at the back of the town', according to which approach route was used. There were proposals for branch lines linking with the Great Western at Slough. And if the Crown maintained its refusal to allow lines to cross the Park, there were plans for bringing the railway as far as Black Potts on the Datchet side of the Thames or the Lord Nelson Inn at Old Windsor, where until 1850 the main road went through the Park to Windsor. There was an almost equally numerous variety of proposals for the London terminus. The site for Waterloo had been acquired in 1844, but the station was not opened until 1848, and Hyde Park Corner, Knightsbridge and Piccadilly all appear in the plans. In the end, however, it all came back to what the Crown would approve. 'It is quite obvious', said the *Express,* 'that the point of Terminus at each end of the Line may be varied or extended at pleasure, according with the wishes of her Majesty's Commissioners of Woods and Forests.'

The Windsor Junction Railway was the project which had the greatest local support and seemed most likely to achieve success. The Company was formed at a. meeting held at the White Hart Inn on 17 October 1844. Incredibly, Dr. Hawtrey, headmaster of Eton College, was voted into the chair. Did the subscribers hope that they would thereby secure his support? If so, they were speedily disillusioned for he made it clear that 'he had attended, as headmaster of Eton College, in order to enable him to watch over the interests of the school, and to secure to him and his successors every facility for protecting the boys under his charge'. None the less a Committee was set up which included Colonel George Alexander Reid of the Life Guards, soon to become one of Windsor's MPs and connected with Nevile Reid's, local brewers and bankers, James Bedborough, Charles Snowden and other members of the Town Council. The Chairman was Captain John Forbes RN, Deputy Lieutenant and Magistrate for Berkshire, and the Secretary, Robert Tighe, Manager of Reid's Brewery and Bank and local historian. Tighe went to Dublin to see the atmospheric railway in operation and returned with a favourable report.

The engineer was Thomas Page, who in the course of a long and distinguished career, was associated with many projects including the Thames Tunnel, the Thames Embankment and Westminster Bridge. Most relevant of all, perhaps, he was acting at this time as consultant engineer to the Crown Commissioners.

Enthusiasm in Windsor itself mounted rapidly. The *Windsor Express* welcomed the project of the Windsor Junction from its inception. 'Our fellow townsmen will doubtless be alive to so important a proposal, and act with zeal and union to promote it'. When other rival plans followed, the *Express* went so far as to say, 'We . . . care not by what party or parties a new line from hence to London is obtained, only hoping that the most direct one that is practicable will be adopted.' The Great Western was also on the alert. Captain Thomas Bulkeley, landowner, magistrate and chief local spokesman for the Company, reported Charles Saunders as saying that it was the intention of the Great Western to make a branch to Windsor, *if they could gain the consent of the Crown.*

The Great Western Company was not popular in Windsor at this time. References to 'this monopolising company' were frequent and the *Express* stated, 'it is not the alteration of the mode of transit from Windsor to the Slough station of the Great Western Railway that is desired by the inhabitants of this town and neighbourhood but a totally distinct line from Windsor to the heart of the Metropolis'.

Everything continued to depend on the good-will of the Crown. Thomas Page was obviously in a good position to gain the ear of the Commissioners and it is clear from remarks at later parliamentary enquiries that the plans of the Windsor

Junction Railway were placed before the Queen. As early, however, as 11 November 1844, the Committee accepted a resolution 'that inasmuch as the Committee, after the greatest diligence and anxiety, have not hitherto obtained the definite consent of the Crown to their undertaking, so as to enable them to proceed to Parliament in the ensuing Session, they have found it necessary to adjourn their further proceedings until the subsequent Session.'

Now followed an interval of more than seven months until another attempt was initiated by a new committee as the outcome of a meeting on 23 June 1845. From the chair Capt. John Forbes placed the position fairly and squarely before the meeting: 'your committee — ascertained that no opinion would be expressed by the Commissioners of Woods and Forests in respect to any project of such important consideration to the Crown as a railway into Windsor, and which may pass over Crown property, until all the plans, sections and surveys were lodged agreeably to the Standing Orders of the House of Commons, and a report made, embracing all the many points affecting the question.' The *Express* summed up the dilemma: 'no railway could go ahead without the Crown's approval; yet the Crown would not approve or disapprove until all plans etc were submitted'.

A full meeting was called at the Guildhall on Wednesday 2 July, with the Mayor, Thomas Clarke, in the chair, and it was decided to make a further approach to the Commissioners 'earnestly soliciting their concurrence in the promotion of one or other of the projected approaches'. On 7 July a letter went to the Earl of Lincoln, the Chief Crown Commissioner, with a request that he would receive a deputation. A reply was received a few days later over the signature of A. Milne, one of the commissioners. It read: 'Sir, on behalf of the Commissioners of HM Woods etc, I have to acknowledge the receipt of your letter of the 7th inst, together with the Memorial and Resolutions of a Meeting of the inhabitants of New Windsor and its neighbourhood, which accompanied it, on the subject of a new direct railway from Windsor to London; and I am to acquaint you that the Board have fully considered this project, in connection with the Crown property at Windsor under their charge and management, and that they are of opinion that such property would be injuriously affected by the proposed railway; and that under these circumstances it will be unnecessary to give the proposed deputation mentioned in your letter the

39

trouble of a conference with this Board.'

Further correspondence followed. The Committee cited the willingness of William IV in 1834 to grant consent for a railway across the Park, and they submitted alternative plans for the consideration of the Crown and expressed their readiness to accept whichever route the Crown preferred. They were prepared to construct a private branch and terminus for the Queen's use, and were willing 'to exchange or remove such roads and buildings as would be conducive to the convenience and privacy of the Castle and the Park and grounds belonging thereto'. All was in vain. A letter from the Commissioners on 13 August brought a final 'no' and the Committee came to the reluctant conclusion that further efforts were useless.

Within a month, however, a new Atmospheric Company — the Windsor, Slough and Staines Atmospheric Railway Company — was formed, with Charles Vignoles as Engineer. The proposal was to build from Windsor Bridge one atmospheric line to the Great Western at Slough by means of a wide curve to the east of Eton, and another via Datchet to Staines to link with the London and South Western. An 18in tube was to be used, with three engine houses, one at Staines, one at Wraysbury and the third on the triangular piece of land at the junction of the lines.

One obvious problem was that of gauges. The Great Western had adopted the broad gauge of 7ft and was obdurate in maintaining it not only on its existing lines but on the new lines it was proposing. Vignoles was so anxious to placate the Great Western, whose co-operation was vital to him, that he seems to have envisaged a broad gauge track on the Slough to Windsor branch. Where this line joined with the narrow gauge track of 4ft 8½in from Staines, provision would have to be made for both gauges for the final approach to Windsor. Vignoles said that the Atmospheric Company would make use of the Great Western Station at Slough or 'rather a siding of that station'. A train arriving at Slough from London would have to be backed on to the Windsor branch, the carriages unhooked and then the Atmospheric would take over. It was proposed that there should be thirty trains a day between Windsor and Slough and twenty between Windsor and Staines. Neither Vignoles nor his colleague Joseph Samuda foresaw any difficulty in connecting the atmospheric line with a locomotive line. But, above all, the railway would 'get rid of noise and smoke and dirt and those things in the vicinity of the Castle'.

This, it was obviously hoped, would overcome one of the main objections of the Crown. The master-stroke was, however, the discovery of a route into Windsor which would not involve Crown land. The key to this route was Romney Island, a long, narrow bank composed mainly of gravel, forming an island or rather two islands — Upper and Lower Romney — half-a-mile in length. From the extremity of the upper island a projection known as the Cobler reaches out towards Windsor Bridge. On the Windsor side of the island is Romney Lock, constructed in 1797; on the other side the main river, with a weir athwart the stream, joining Romney to another island on the Eton side. The plan was to bring the railway from the north bank near Black Potts by a bridge to Romney Island, which it would traverse by means of a wooden viaduct. When it reached the upper end it would then cross to the Windsor bank by another bridge and so continue to the terminal station beneath the walls of the Castle.

How handy for the Court! Throughout the previous year foreign princes had come to Windsor — the Tsar of Russia, the King and Queen of the French, the King and Queen of the Belgians and the King of Saxony had all stayed at the Castle. Sir Robert Peel, with Lady Peel, came frequently, as did not only members of Peel's Cabinet, but Opposition notables such as Melbourne, Russell and Palmerston. The *Court Intelligence* gives an impression of an almost unending stream of visiting Royals, diplomats and statesmen. Many travelled by way of Paddington and Slough and returned to London the same way. The Queen and Prince Albert had taken their first journey together by train from Slough to Paddington on 13 June 1842, and after that initial venture, they used the railway regularly. Like the meanest of their subjects, however, they had first to travel to Slough by road — even if they travelled in style. with an escort of Household Cavalry. And when they reached Paddington, again they had to travel by carriage through the streets of London to Buckingham Palace or the City. If they wanted to go to Osborne, their newly acquired residence in the Isle of Wight, they had to travel by road eighteen miles to Farnborough before they could proceed by rail. What a boon the new railway would be! As Charles Vignoles and Joseph Samuda conceived their new railway they must have had visions of the Queen and her Prince, along with all the great of the land, travelling happily on the Atmospheric.

41

The Crown, however, remained silent in the face of the new proposals. The promoters were obviously placing their faith in the Romney Island route and as a consequence were less anxious to defer to the Crown. Richard Sharman, by then retired after many years of service on the Council, had said at a meeting at the Guildhall in September that 'though willing to pay all proper respect to authority, he thought that the present was an occasion to which even authority ought to bow'. This sentiment was echoed by many who wanted the railway and resented the negative attitude of the Crown.

In the following weeks the forces on either side ranged themselves for battle. The Great Western gave no sign of being willing to co-operate. Saunders in fact 'solemnly assured' Eton that 'nothing whatever should prevent the GW people from straining every nerve to secure the defeat or withdrawal of the Bill'.

The College took its usual line of unyielding opposition. Following a meeting at the Christopher Inn – to which the press and public were not admitted – with Dr. Hawtrey in the chair, the College petitioned Parliament against the project. After reciting the details of the safeguarding clause of 1835 'prohibiting the introduction of any railway by any company or person within three miles of the college of Eton, without the consent of your petitioners in writing, under their corporate seal', the Petition continued: 'That such prohibitory clause was so inserted in the Great Western Railway Act, for the express purpose of preventing further interference with the privacy, discipline and safety of the College and school, and to ensure to the scholars undisturbed application to their studies, and the uninterrupted enjoyment of their wonted recreation. Whereas the effect of the proposed bill will be to bring all the contemplated evils within a few yards only of the college, school and playing grounds'.

A severe flood in January 1846 added strength to the College opposition. On the 28th, declared the Petition, 'the whole of the playing fields of the College were under water, and the flood washed the walls of the out-offices, and came within 27 yards of the south-east walls of the College . . . The embankment, bridge and other works necessary to form and construct the railway would cause such an obstruction to the waters, and pen them up in such a manner as to subject the College to the most destructive consequences'. One Etonian expressed anxiety

42

to Batcheldor at the delay in presenting the College Petition. 'The waters are subsiding fast', he wrote, in obvious apprehension that once the flood danger was past the impact of the Petition would be less.

The *Windsor Express,* on the other hand, excelled itself in extolling the virtues of the new railway. Previously the emphasis had been on what the railway would look like from the Castle or the College. The *Express* changed the emphasis and described what the Castle and the College would look like from the railway: 'the approach to Windsor by the viaduct will not only afford a most beautiful view of the Castle, with its majestic keep and machicolated towers on the one side, and Eton College with its "Antique towers, That crown the watery glade", on the other, but the viaduct will of itself . . . be a most pleasing and picturesque object, particularly from the College, passing as it will on the opposite side of the water; and when the Park wall is removed, as we understand is contemplated, the view across the viaduct of the Park and Castle will form a most interesting and harmonious coup d'oeil'.

The *Express* had nothing but contempt for the attitude of the Great Western and of Eton. The opposition of the former, it said, was 'natural enough — to that company the convenience of the inhabitants or the prosperity of the town are as dust in the balance, when weighed against the financial considerations'. The Petition from the College was dismissed as 'this choice morceau of barefaced mendacity . . . got up for no other purpose than to mystify the minds of Old Etonians, and convert into a prejudice the very natural feelings of veneration, with which, doubtless, all or most of them regard the scenes of their boyhood'.

The Windsor Council also gave the project their blessing. Several leading members of the Council were among the sponsors. It was said that James Bedborough 'originated this line down Romney Island' and John Secker, the Town Clerk, was asked at the parliamentary enquiry if the projected railway was not in fact known as 'the Bedborough line', to which he replied, rather starchily, 'I have never heard it so called'. When, at their meeting on New Year's Day, 1846, the Town Clerk reported the receipt of notices of a number of railway bills, the Council came down in favour of the Windsor, Slough and Staines Atmospheric Railway by eight votes to four and a Petition went forward to Parliament accordingly.

The previous project, that of the Windsor Junction Railway, had never reached Parliament, because its promoters had felt it essential to secure the approval of the Crown first — and, as we have seen, this approval was not forthcoming. The new proposals were embodied in a Bill which received its First Reading in the Commons on 13 February 1846 and its Second a week later. It was then remitted to the Select Committee on Railway Bills, consisting of four MPs, together with Mr. Southeron, MP for North Wilts., as Chairman. The Committee did not reach the Bill until after the Easter Recess; it finally met on nine days between 5 May, and the 19th, each sitting normally beginning at noon.

The large committee room would be filled with MPs, lawyers, witnesses, maybe other interested parties, along with attendants, clerks and shorthand writers. The last took down every word and afterwards wrote up the evidence in longhand. The MPs who formed the Committee, apart from an occasional question or comment, for the most part listened to the evidence in silence. The lawyers, on the other hand, questioned and cross-examined as if time was no object, going round repetitively in apparently endless circles, seeking to trap witnesses into contradicting themselves or each other, or making an admission which would be damaging to their cause.

Surprisingly little time was taken up with a discussion of the merits and demerits of atmospheric traction. There was almost an agreement to disagree. Vignoles was asked: 'don't you know in point of fact that this is a bad system?' To which he replied, 'no, I deny it altogether. I think it is a very good system'. There was some adverse comment on the working of the London and Croydon Atmospheric Railway, which had begun to operate a public service in the previous January. The counsel cross-examining Vignoles claimed that locomotives were kept in readiness and sometimes had to be used when 'the atmospheric is gone'. He tried to show that 'the atmospheric principle' was unproven and asked, 'do you think it prudent as an engineer to apply it to another line until it is?' Vignoles replied with complete self-assurance: 'I can see my way quite clear to the development of it'.

If there was any admission of possible failure, it was that, although the line was based upon the atmospheric principle, it was capable of being worked by locomotive. Almost, in the same breath, however, Vignoles posed the alternative possibility that, between Staines and London, locomotive traction might be changed to atmospheric. In the climate of thought at the time Vignoles like many others was convinced that the atmospheric principle would 'produce a revolution in the whole system of railway construction and traffic, and in the end be universally adopted'.

The most serious practical objection to the railway was the possibility that it would increase the danger of the floods that inundated the low-lying land every winter. The narratives of the period show that scarcely a year passed without large portions of the Home Park, the Eton playing fields, the Brocas, Runnymede being under water. There had been particularly severe floods in 1809, 1822, 1836 and as recently as January 1846; on all of these occasions many houses in Windsor and Eton had been flooded.

The Committee spent many hours in hearing evidence on this subject. The evidence of George Treacher, Surveyor of the Thames Navigation Commissioners, — specially summoned by Speaker's Order — alone covers more than one hundred pages and is devoted almost exclusively to the problems of flooding in relation to the project. Almost every witness who appeared in support of the Bill was grilled on the subject. What would be the effect of the viaduct and the two bridges that would carry the railway across the Thames? Would there be embankments? How high would the viaduct be? What would be the distance between the piles?

Vignoles in particular was emphatic that the construction of the railway would not increase the flood danger. The piles of the viaduct would be at least forty feet apart. The bridge from the Cobler to the Windsor bank would be a timber bridge similar in construction to the one at the other end of Romney Island, with two large 100ft spans. Much of the blame for the severity of the floods was placed upon the fact that the weir was 'at right angles across the river'; it was proposed to alter the direction of the weir so that it would cross the river diagonally.

As for the operation of the railway being affected by floods, this was impossible. Vignoles said that the lowest part of the railway would be 2ft 6in above the highest flood level, namely that of 1836. None the less Counsel could not refrain from conjuring up a picture of what the effect would be if the flood water flowed over the atmospheric pipes. Would it 'give rather an *asthmatic* touch to the pipes'?

We have seen that the promoters believed that by using Romney Island they had found a way of reaching Windsor without passing over Crown land. Henry Darvill, the local solicitor for the Company, gave a categorical assurance that this was so and claimed that the consent of the Crown was not necessary to the Bill.

The Counsel for the opposition, however, found two possible points of objection and made the most of them. The Castle Water Works were on the bank opposite Romney Island and from the Works a pipe or conduit passed under the Island — at a depth, so it was stated, of 15ft. So, if the railway traversed the Island, it must pass over the pipe and therefore over Crown property!

Secondly, it was contended that the railway could not be carried from Romney Island to the terminal station near the bridge without affecting Crown property. This was so clouded in doubt that the opponents of the Bill at one point fell back on the argument that the ownership of the river bed — or of undefined parts of the river bed — was vested in the Crown and that one of the piles of the bridge which would bring the railway from the Island to the Windsor bank would as a consequence rest on Crown land.

This was hair-splitting with a vengeance — not that it worried the lawyers! What had more point perhaps was the threat to the privacy of the Castle and its occupants. Twice the subject of the bathing habits of Prince Albert was brought up. Edward Jesse, Surveyor of HM Parks and Palaces, who was attending the enquiry in what he insisted was an unofficial capacity, was asked with reference to the bathing place near the weir, 'do you not know Prince Albert is in the habit of leaving the Castle and walking down there frequently in the summer to bathe from Datchet lane up to this water bathing place?' Jesse answered, 'I heard he did when he first came to reside at Windsor. I do not think he has the last year or two'. And then followed a further question, 'Do you know whether Prince Albert is in the habit of exercising his greyhound in that part of the Home Park which is near the bathing place?' Jesse's reply was a simple, 'I have not heard of it'.

So learned counsel did not get very much change out of Edward Jesse, but another line of argument was certainly clever, perhaps rather too clever to carry conviction. Great attention, as we have seen, was focussed on the problems of bringing the Railway along Romney Island and its liability to flooding. The engineers demonstrated that the viaduct and therefore the Railway would be well above the flood levels of recent years. If that is so, the lawyers intervened triumphantly, the trains passing along the viaduct would be higher than the park wall and 'will enable those fortunate peepers to see all that is going on'.

The question of noise nuisance was difficult to establish, since one of the great advantages of atmospheric over locomotive traction was the lack of noise. But if the trains were silent, there was still the engine house. True, it was on the north bank of the river, at least a mile from the Castle — and, being to the north-east, in the opposite direction to the prevailing winds. You could not, however, expect to have a 150hp engine without noise. And even if the engine could not be *heard* from the Castle, at least its house could be *seen*. It would be an eyesore to Her Majesty. Samuda answered, 'I think it may be made ornamental' — no doubt with Norman Romanesque or perhaps Tudor Gothic in mind, on which Counsel commented, 'So the Chimney Sweep said of the Chimney Pot'.

So every possible argument in defence of the 'privacy and comfort' of the Crown was exploited to the full. Even the fisheries might be disturbed — and then what might not happen to the 'perch and gudgeon for the Queen's table'? Yet in a sense the defence of the Crown's interests was almost completely vicarious. No Counsel represented the Crown. There were witnesses associated with it — Edward Jesse, James Simpson, Civil Engineer, Woods and Forests, for twenty five years; Edward Leigh Pemberton, Solicitor for Woods and Forests; Thomas Page, Engineer for the 1844 Atmospheric project and former consultant engineer to Woods and Forests. None of these, however, came in an official capacity as representing the Crown; some indeed had been subpoened by Speaker's Order to appear as witnesses. Yet the unseen presence of the Crown pervaded the Enquiry.

The presence of Eton College was, on the other hand, very far from unseen. The College, not only in this but in every Enquiry, deployed its heavy artillery against any threat to its interests. At the opening of the Enquiry it was revealed that Romney Island had recently been purchased by Eton College from the Commissioners of the Thames Navigation. Counsel contended that the purchase was to improve protection against floods and 'for the purpose of preventing any nuisance, and adding to the privacy and security of the college and playing grounds'. John Secker, however, had no doubt in his own mind what the motive was — 'I have heard that the College bought it for the purpose of opposing this Railway certainly'. Eton's purchase of Romney Island angered the promoters of the Atmospheric Railway. At the time of the Parliamentary Enquiry H. Darvill, local solicitor to the railway company, wrote to Batcheldor: 'Dear Sir, I will thank you to be prepared to produce before the Committee on Monday next all the deeds, papers and documents mentioned in the Notice served on you.

'My clerk informs me that when served with the Notice you stated you would not produce the conveyance from the Thames Navigation Commissioners and I therefore think it right to apprize you that you will be called upon to produce it and the other documents mentioned in the Notice'. Curiously, the subject never seems to have been raised again during the Enquiry. But Romney Island, though within Windsor, is today still the property of Eton College.

The principal witness for the College was the headmaster himself, Dr. Edward Hawtrey. He made the concession that the College might consent to certain lines well away from College property. He would not object to a line entering Windsor from the south — the side of the Castle away from Eton. If a railway from Slough to Windsor became inevitable, the College might consent if it was 'beyond that part which is occupied by the boys in their play'. Really, however, 'the College did not wish for the railway at all' and certainly the line proposed in the Atmospheric Bill was anathema. At its nearest point the railway would be only 215 yards from the main buildings of the College. It crossed a corner of the 'shooting field', which was a part of the College playing fields. So, from the point of view of the College, the proposal was completely objectionable.

Dr. Hawtrey had no illusions about the nature of the boys under his charge. In the construction stage there would be the danger of confrontation between the boys and the 'navigators', a confrontation which the headmaster explained would mean 'disputes with men of violent characters who may not be able to take with patience any slight ill-treatment, or laughter, or ill-usage they may meet with from young boys'.

If in spite of the dangers implicit in this situation, the railway project was carried through, another peril would arise. 'Everybody who knows what Eton Boys are', said Dr. Hawtrey, 'must be aware there are circumstances occur to induce boys to throw stones when carriages are going rapidly by'. This would 'become a favourite trial of skill within a very short time as to how soon a stone would penetrate through two windows at once'. Pressed on this point, the Headmaster expressed his belief, 'I think the love of breaking windows is innate in all boys'.

As an interesting comment on Dr. Hawtrey's views, the *Windsor Express* in its issue of 13 May 1875 — nearly 30 years later — reported an incident in which the royal train containing the Princess of Wales and her children was stoned as it passed over the Eton Wick Road bridge. One stone broke the glass of the saloon in which the royal party was seated and a piece of glass hit the Princess. The report continued, 'we can say this is not the first time stones have been thrown at trains on this section of the Windsor to Slough railway line. Dr. Hornby, the headmaster of Eton, states that if the culprits should be found to be boys of the College they will be flogged with the utmost severity and then expelled'.

Probably the project for a Windsor, Slough and Staines Atmospheric Railway was foredoomed to failure. This was not primarily due to doubts about the atmospheric principle. As we have seen, these occupied only a small part of the attention of the Enquiry. The shortcomings of the atmospheric system were shown up clearly over the next year or two and the hopes entertained of this 'mechanical might-have-been' quickly faded. The South Devon Railway showed some of the failings; the leather flap swelled in wet weather, shrivelled in hot weather and in some places became detached from the tube. Thus the tube became difficult to seal. Robert Stephenson, who had consistently opposed the atmospheric system, emphasised the operating disadvantages of inflexibility such as inability to reverse a train, put it in a siding or cope with an accident.

Fundamentally, however, the reason for the defeat of the Windsor Atmospheric project was that it did not receive the support of the Crown, Eton College, or the Great Western.

So, at the ninth and final sitting of the Parliamentary Committee on 19 May, the Chairman announced that they had decided not to hear further evidence. The Atmospheric Bill had had a hearing, but the final verdict of the Committee that 'they were strongly of opinion that they ought not to recommend Parliament to sanction the line' had an air of inevitability about it.

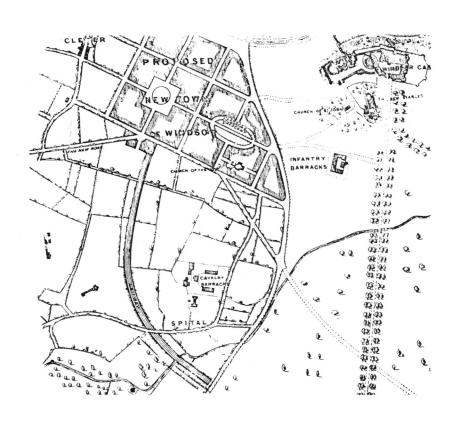

ABOVE: In this 1847 plan for a new Windsor, separated from the Castle by a belt of open land, a railway is brought by a tunnel under the Park and the Long Walk to emerge at the back of the town.

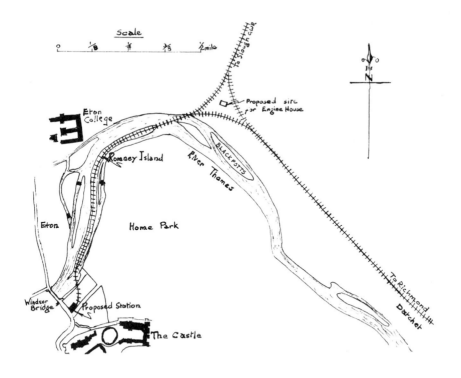

Scale

0   ⅛   ¼   ⅜   ½ mile

To Slough Spur

N

Eton College

Proposed site for Engine House

Romney Island

River Thames

BLACKPOTTS

Eton

Home Park

To Richmond

Datchet

Windsor Bridge

Proposed Station

The Castle

ABOVE: The Windsor, Slough and Staines Atmospheric Railway, 1845-46, showing the proposed routes in the vicinity of Windsor and Eton, especially the use of Romney Island. BELOW: A contemporary print of sections of the South Devon Railway, constructed by Brunel, one of the most famous of the atmospheric railways to operate. (BR)

51

ABOVE: Contemporary print of sections of the South Devon Atmospheric Railway. (BR) BELOW: 'An eyesore to her Majesty'? An engine house on the S. Devon railway, perhaps similar to those proposed for the Windsor railway.

WINDSOR, SLOUGH, AND STAINES ATMOSPHERIC RAILWAY.

CAPITAL, £150,000,

IN 7,500 SHARES, OF £20 EACH.—DEPOSIT, £2 2s. PER SHARE.

Provisionally Registered pursuant to 7 and 8 Vic., c. 110.

Provisional Committee.

JOHN RAMSBOTTOM, Esq., M.P. *for Windsor.*
RALPH NEVILLE, Esq., M.P. *for Windsor.*
JAMES THOMAS BEDBOROUGH, Esq., *Upton Park, near Windsor.*
JEREMIAH PILCHER, Esq., *Russell-square, late Sheriff of London, Director of the Paris and Strasbourg Railway.*
LEWIS POCOCK, Esq., *Montague-street, Russell-square, Director of the Reading and Reigate Railway, and the Argus Life Assurance Company.*
JOHN EDWARDS LANGTON, Esq., *Maidenhead.*
FREDERICK FOWLER, Esq., *Windsor.*
JOSEPH CARRINGTON RIDGWAY, Esq., *Roehampton Lodge, Surrey, one of the Provisional Committee of the Exeter, Dorchester, and Weymouth Junction Coast Railway.*
JOHN FOWLER, Esq., *Southleys House, Datchet.*
SIR RAYMOND JARVIS, *Fair Oak Park, Winchester.*

VALENTINE KNIGHT, Esq., 3, *Cornwall Terrace, Regent's Park.*
WILLIAM VERNON STEPHENS, Esq., *Birkins Manor House, Horton.*
WILLIAM BERRIDGE, Esq., *Windsor.*
JOHN BRADLEY SHUTTLEWORTH, Esq., 33, *Eastcheap, London.*
CALEB NORRIS, Esq., *Lancaster-place, London, one of the Provisional Committee of the Exeter, Dorchester, and Weymouth Junction Coast Railway.*
RICHARD IBOTSON, Esq., *Poyle Mills, near Horton.*
ALFRED FOWLER, Esq., *Datchet, Bucks.*
ROBERT OWEN ALAND, Esq., *Greek-street, Soho.*
SAMUEL DAVIS, Esq., *Brunswick Terrace, Windsor.*
MR. JOHN ROBERTS, *Windsor.*
MR. WILLIAM HENRY BURGE, *Windsor.*
MR. WILLIAM WEAVER BERRIDGE, *Windsor.*
MR. JOHN CLODE, Jun., *Windsor.*

WITH POWER TO ADD TO THEIR NUMBER.

Engineer.
CHARLES VIGNOLES, ESQ., F.R.A.S. M.R.I.A.

Solicitors.
MESSRS. DARVILL & GEARY, WINDSOR.

Bankers.
MESSRS. WILLIAMS, DEACON, & Co., LONDON. | MESSRS. NEVILE REID & Co., WINDSOR.

Secretary, pro tem.
MR. HENRY COOK, WINDSOR.

PROSPECTUS.

THIS Railway is intended to remedy the great inconvenience and delay at present existing in the communication between the towns of Windsor and Eton, and the Great Western Railway, and also to obtain the advantages proposed by the Staines and Richmond Lines of Railway to a London Terminus at Hungerford Bridge, with such other facilities as may be opened up by any of the proposed Lines proceeding from the West-end of London towards Windsor.

Prospectus of the Windsor, Slough and Staines Atmospheric Railway, 1845.

53

WINDSOR, SLOUGH, AND STAINES
ATMOSPHERIC RAILWAY.

OPPOSED by the Provost and Fellows of the College Royal of Eton, near Windsor.

Chief Points on which they rest their Opposition, as more fully insisted on in their Petition against the Bill.

FIRST.—Because the approach of the proposed Railway within a few yards of the Playing Fields of the College, will inflict permanent and irremediable evil on the School in all its relations of discipline, study, and recreation, by affecting the privacy of its position and the security of the Scholars; who will be disturbed in the exercise of their wonted amusements; and incur serious inconvenience, if not danger, by the rise of the waters in consequence of the embankment on Romney Island, and of the Bridge or Viaduct to be erected near the Oak Tree in the Playing Fields.

SECONDLY.—Because the Railway will, by its peculiar construction of a Bridge or Viaduct *up*, rather than *across*, the Thames, injure the property of the College, and destroy some of its most important immunities there, beyond the reach of any compensation; and by its probable effect in altering the bed and current of the Stream, impede the navigation of the River.

THIRDLY.—Because the necessary consequence of the proposed Works, Bridge or Viaduct, and Embankments will be to dam and pen up the waters in such manner as to subject the College, and its adjoining Lands and Playing Fields, to extensive inundations, calculated to inflict the most injurious consequences on the Buildings of the College, and exposing the Scholars to much danger.

FOURTHLY.—Because it will be proved in evidence that all the purposes of the proposed Railway between Windsor and Slough, might be better answered by a Line passing entirely on the western side of Eton, crossing the River some distance above Windsor Bridge; which Line would not injure the navigation of the River, nor, if properly constructed, present any obstruction to the Flood Waters, and would pass through property of considerably less value, and avoid the necessity of interfering with Lands immediately connected with the College.

FIFTHLY.—Because the expense of the proposed Railway will far exceed the estimates; and

Part of an Eton College statement in opposition to the Atmospheric Railway.

54

BATTLE OF THE COMPANIES

The failure of the Windsor, Slough and Staines Atmospheric Railway Bill left the field clear for the two great companies – the Great Western and the South Western.

The battle had already been joined for 'possession' of the south and south-west. The plan of the original 'London and Southampton' to reach Bristol from Basingstoke by way of Bath had come to naught and the Great Western was pushing out tentacles southwards from its main line. The rivalry was intensified as a result of the 'gauge war' – the broad gauge of the Western versus the narrow gauge of the South Western. Nowhere was the confrontation more bitter than at Windsor. Each company regarded the other as 'the enemy'.

In Windsor itself there was a speedy acceptance of the need to go in with either the Great Western *or* the South Western. But which? The Great Western was the first in the field and so the first inclination of the shareholders of the Atmospheric Company was to go in with them rather than with the newly formed South Western. A meeting of shareholders which took place at the Town Hall on 16 July 1846 was recommended that 'the company be dissolved and that their amalgamation with the Great Western Company be consented to'. The chair was taken by Ralph Neville, one of Windsor's MPs, who said that, when he was appointed Chairman in the previous January, he considered that the first duty imposed on him was to make known the wishes of the friends of the scheme to the Crown Commissioners. He had an interview with the Earl of Lincoln, then Chief Commissioner, who promised to give consideration to the proposals. On 16 March his Lordship said that the Crown 'had an objection to the contemplated line passing over Romney Island'. This suggested that there was more hope in going along with the Great Western proposals for a branch line from Slough to Windsor terminating 'somewhere near George Street'. Neville said that he had heard both Lord Lincoln and Lord Canning (Lincoln's successor) speak of the necessity there existed for a railway to Windsor. It was also suggested that Eton College was prepared to approve. (From this time until the Windsor railways finally received parliamentary approval a distinction has to be made between the College and the School. The Provost and the Fellows, who were the College authorities, were prepared to give conditional assent to the Great Western; the headmaster and masters, supported by many Old Etonians, maintained their opposition to the end.)

The *Express,* however, was consistently hostile to the Great Western proposals. Great play was still being made of the fact that the Great Western line did not go into the centre of London, but only to Paddington which was a mere suburb. In this the *Express* echoed public opinion in the town. W. Chadwick said at a meeting of shareholders on 5 August that 'what the people of Windsor wanted in the way of railway communication with the metropolis was a line that would give them what the Great Western did not possess — a central terminus in London'.

As the outcome of a series of meetings in August and September support for the South Western steadily grew. True, there were still supporters for the Great Western. One of these was Col. Alexander Reid, Neville's colleague as MP, who was before long to switch his allegiance to the South Western and become one of its most energetic advocates. Another was Henry Darvill, who became solicitor for the Great Western. He summed up the attitude of the 'higher powers' as 'we don't want a railway into Windsor, but if we have one it shall be the Great Western'. So, he argued, to attempt to amalgamate with the South Western would end in failure. Darvill also made the point that the Great Western route to London was shorter than any South Western route could be.

Darvill and Bedborough, Liberal colleagues on the Council and often staunch allies in local politics, came to differ violently on the railway question. Darvill had supported the Atmospheric project and was credited with drafting the Council's Petition in its support. Once, however, his professional interests linked him with the Great Western, he used his considerable oratorical skill in its favour.

Bedborough said at the meeting on 5 August, 'the present plan was got up between the Great Western Company and Eton College'. He referred to the statement made at the July meeting that the Earl of Lincoln had objected to a railroad going over Romney Island and commented that 'the objection of his Lord-

56

ship sprang more from his feelings as an Old Etonian than from his inclinations as Chief Commissioner of Her Majesty's Woods and Forests', a comment that was greeted with a chorus of 'hear, hear's.

A resolution was moved by W. Chadwick, seconded by W.H. Burge, 'That this meeting, thinking it desirable for the inhabitants of Windsor that they should have a better terminus in London than that afforded by the Great Western at Paddington, do resolve that a deputation be appointed to treat with the South Western and to report thereon to a meeting to be held in the Town Hall, Windsor, on Wednesday, the 19th inst.'

By 19 August a meeting with the South Western had taken place, but there had been insufficient time to reach decisions. So, although a resolution was proposed advocating union with the South Western, it was eventually agreed to adjourn for a fortnight. By the time the adjourned meeting was held on 2 September considerable progress had been made, so that, with James Bedborough in the chair, it was now agreed to give full backing to the South Western. The proposal also included the provision of a line from Windsor to Slough by a joint arrangement with the Great Western, obviously with a single terminus in Windsor.

The report stated that 'the deputation also sought and obtained the honour of an interview with the Commissioners of Woods and Forests to whom they submitted the proposed alteration of the approach into Windsor, by passing to the east of Eton; and the deputation have the gratification to state that Lord Morpeth [the new Chief Crown Commissioner] and other members of the Board expressed themselves favourably towards the plan submitted to them, and authorised the deputation to report that the Board did not express any objection to any part of the proposed plan. They have also to report that Mr. Page, the engineer to the Board, was present and stated to the Commissioners that he considered the proposed line near Eton would be favourably received by the Provost and Fellows of Eton College'.

Interest in Windsor continued to mount. The *Express* supported the South Western vigorously and when, on 22 September, a further meeting was held at the Town Hall, Bedborough was able, as Chairman, to report further progress in the arrangements with the South Western Company. There were still the doubting Thomases. Would not Eton oppose? Would not the

57

Great Western oppose? To the latter Bedborough replied, 'the case was materially different to what it was in the late defeat of the Windsor, Slough and Staines line. Then the opposition was by a great company against a little one; but now, on the contrary, it would be between two great companies. The South Western might fearlessly meet the Great Western'.

The answer to the query about the attitude of the College – or at least of the Eton masters – was given at a meeting at the beginning of October. Dr. Hawtrey was present and vehement opposition was expressed to the new proposals, in fact to any railway proposals. Edward Coleridge asserted that 'a railway so near Eton as that in contemplation would entirely destroy the character of the place'. A motion to oppose all railways passing through the parish of Eton was carried unanimously and a committee was set up 'to watch all railway proceedings in connection with Eton'.

This meeting was reported in the *Express* on 10 October 1846. In the next two issues, 17 and 24 October, the *Express* carried the Prospectus (dated 14 October 1846) of the new railway which would 'proceed from Staines by way of Wraysbury and Datchet to Windsor, the terminus at which town will be made in the locality most approved of by Her Majesty's Commissioners of Woods and Forests and by the authorities of Eton College'. This probably meant acceptance of the fact that the railway would only be allowed to come as far as Datchet – or Black Potts – in the first instance, but left the door open for an extension to Windsor if permission was granted.

Obviously at this time discussions were proceeding with the Commissioners of Woods and Forests. A deputation from the Directors of the Windsor, Staines and South Western Railway had an interview with Lord Morpeth on Tuesday, 3 October, at the Office of the Woods and Forests in Whitehall Place. The deputation consisted of Col. Reid MP, Mr. Lacy, Mr. Bedborough, Mr. Chadwick, Mr. Horn (SW Secretary) and Mr. Drake (SW solicitor). On the following day a deputation consisting of Capt. Bulkeley, Chairman of the Windsor Railway (the proposed Great Western branch from Slough to Windsor), C. Russell (Chairman of the Great Western), Messrs. Fowler, Davis, Roberts and Darvill from Windsor and Mr. Saunders, Secretary of the Great Western, had a similar interview.

While the formal notices were being lodged and plans deposited, preparations were being made for a public meeting to discuss the rival merits of the SW and the GW projected lines of railway. The meeting took place at the Town Hall on Monday, 7 December, and proved to be the stormiest in the long series of railway meetings. 'We never remember to have seen the Town Hall so crowded', commented the *Express*. James Bedborough, now Mayor, took the chair. Several MPs were present, along with Saunders of the Great Western and Locke of the South Western. There appears no question that the accusation that the Great Western attempted to pack the meeting was justified. 'In the body of the meeting', reported the *Express*, 'were observed a large number of GWR Company's employees — clerks, check-takers, constables, and even navigators ("dressed-up navigators", the *Express* described them in a later reference), who had been sent to the town during the morning, the road to which had been distinguished by the continual traffic of omnibuses, cabs and flys from the Slough station in order to deposit their contents in Windsor, and which imparted to the road through Eton the appearance of an Ascot race-day. Nothing indeed had been neglected for facilitating the extent of supply by this monopolizing company; even the express up-train (a thing unprecedented) had been allowed to stop at Slough; and there was, moreover, a special train from London to deposit persons to attend the meeting on behalf of the company. The consequence of this great influx of strangers, who at an early hour congregated in the Hall, was the exclusion from the place and meeting of a great number of the residents of the town and neighbourhood'.

The meeting began at nine o'clock with an opening statement by the Chairman. A resolution was then proposed supporting the South Western project. The proposer, Samuel Minton, said that 'he had the greatest satisfaction in assuring the meeting, from authority, that the Commissioners of Woods and Forests had no objection to offer on the part of the Government to the South Western'. The resolution was seconded by John Clode, junior, a leading Liberal in the town and Mayor at the time of Napoleon III's visit to Windsor in 1855. The speeches of both proposer and seconder were punctuated by continual cries of 'No, no' from the Great Western people, 'who had packed the meeting, and were paid for their attendance'.

Captain Bulkeley then proposed an amendment in favour of the Great Western. He made the point that the South Western would stop at Black Potts, whereas the Great Western aimed at a terminus *in Windsor*. 'He had no hesitation in apprising the meeting that a *bribe* had been given by the South Western Company to HM Government for the purpose of attaining the assent of the Crown . . . He had himself put the question to Lord Morpeth, by whom it was not denied that they had offered to contribute a certain sum towards carrying out the improvements meditated the Department of Woods and Forests'.

Despite disorderly interruptions the procedure at least had been in order. The resolution in favour of the South Western had been proposed and seconded; the amendment in favour of the Great Western had also been duly proposed and seconded. Sooner or later, however, a vote must be taken. Here the Chairman was in an obvious dilemma. At this point Bedborough said that, 'before he put the amendment, he had to request that none but those persons who resided in the neighbourhood of Windsor, Eton and Clewer would join in a show of hands'. This ruling resulted in pandemonium. When Bedborough was able to continue, he repeated that no one but those living in the neighbourhood had any right to take part in the proceedings. A large proportion of the people at the meeting were strangers, and he therefore hoped that whatever decision was come to, it would be the decision of the inhabitants of Windsor, Eton. Clewer and the neighbourhood. Once more there was uproar. Representatives of the Great Western party strongly insisted that it was a public meeting at which the public had a right to attend.

Eventually the discussion was able to continue. Several speakers, including Ralph Neville, MP for Windsor, and William Hayter, MP for Wells, attempted to make themselves heard, but what they had to say was largely drowned by an 'organised volley of hisses, groans, whistling and bellowing'.

When the Mayor put the amendment the Great Western party voted in spite of his ruling, many holding up both hands in favour of the amendment. To the accompaniment of great cheering and tumult, the Mayor declared the amendment carried. At this George Long, a local solicitor, was heard to say, 'I demand a poll' – but no decision was taken at this point. Instead, following the vote in favour of the Great Western, the adoption of a Petition supporting the vote was moved by Captain Bulkeley, seconded by Rev. M'Croa, Independent minister in Windsor. This brought the Eton contingent to their feet in protest. Cookesley opposed the Great Western and proposed the rejection of the petition. 'He said', reported the *Express,* 'that the line proposed would inflict a grievous wrong on Eton . . . It passes by the Brocas where the town of Eton had rights of enjoyment from time immemorial. It destroys the hockey fields, and cuts up the Brocas clump.' He brought in the now familiar arguments about increased danger of flooding and the threat to the privacy of the College bathing place. 'He would promise them the combined hostility of the Eton masters and the Eton men, who would spend their last shilling and their best energies in resisting an unjust and unnecessary aggression'. Charles Stuart Voules, Windsor solicitor, who himself had three sons at Eton, seconded the rejection of the petition. Coleridge supported them — 'he felt the melancholy conviction that great evils would ensue to Eton if the Great Western scheme were allowed to proceed. He called upon all the parents of the Eton boys to arrest this absurd destruction of all they should regard and value.' By this time Bedborough had had enough. He declined to sign the petition, proposed a poll and declared the meeting closed.

The *Express* report continues: 'The meeting broke up in confusion, after a sitting of five hours, one hour of which was spent in darkness, and two hours in the most disorderly and disgraceful uproar. The Town Hall emptied by degrees; but the public houses became simultaneously full. There were 'treats' and 'spreads' provided with tolerable profusion, as we learn, by Great Western generosity for the distant way-farers summoned to do their bidding, and the end was worthy of the commencement. If the first act exhibited the bustle of a race course, the curtain dropped on one of those scenes observed at rotten boroughs at elections, where it is deemed requisite to overwhelm public opinion with factious votes, or to subborn the basest appetites of dependents, for the purpose of obtaining a corrupt and false majority'.

The poll took place on the five following days, Tuesday to Saturday, between twelve and one o'clock each day. The *Express* says that only residents present at Monday's meeting were allowed to vote — though this must at least have included those who, failing to gain admission to the main Guildhall Chamber, crowded the vestibule, stairways and possibly the Corn Exchange below. The result of the poll was decisive — 14 for the Great Western Petition and 238 against.

After this dramatic confrontation, there appears to have been something of a lull. Both the Great Western and the South Western promoted bills and the preparation and the formalities followed a measured but slow course. The one man who never paused in his activity was James Bedborough. As soon as be became Mayor in November 1846 he made the promotion of the railway project his first concern. At the Council meeting on 5 December — two days before the public meeting at the Guildhall — the General Purposes Committee was requested to watch all developments and to report on them to the Council. The proposals for town improvements promoted by the Crown had by this time become intertwined with the railway proposals and at their meeting on 1 March 1847 the Council surveyed the whole situation and agreed to the dispatch of two Petitions to the Houses of Parliament, one in support of the Town Improvements and the second in support of the South Western railway proposals. This decision had been preceded by the usual sharp debate. Robert Blunt, the veteran Tory leader of the Council, made a long speech on the advantages of the South Western line. Calling Windsor 'a holiday town', he emphasised the fact that the South Western line did not necessitate any destruction, whereas the Great Western required the demolition of 63 houses. He did not think it mattered if the South Western terminus was at Black Potts, Henry Darvill, moving an amendment in favour of the Great Western branch line — or, strictly speaking, to consider both lines — made an even longer speech, answering all the points made by Blunt. The speech occupies nearly a column of small print in the *Express* and rises to the level of oratory. No other member of the Council could speak with the eloquence that seemed to come naturally to Darvill. He argued the convenience of a central station; it would be advantageous to the town to get rid of 'one of the greatest nuisances the town contains' (a reference to the George Street slum); the Great Western promised a quicker service. There were acrimonious exchanges between Darvill and Bedborough. The role of an impartial chairman was never one that commended itself to Bedborough. He spoke himself, re-iterating such familiar arguments such as the South Western line would penetrate further into London than the Great Western at Paddington. Darvill rose to reply. This was not to the liking of the Council, but he was eventually 'heard in explanation'. Darvill's amendment was then put to the vote and defeated by 10 votes to 3, with three abstentions. The original motion was then put and carried on a show of hands.

The Railway Petition, in addition to re-emphasising the greater convenience of the various termini of the South Western railway in proximity to the Houses of Parliament, the Courts of Law, the City, and all the southern parts of London, introduced two further points, never made so explicitly before. It would lay open 'a direct approach . . . to the counties of Kent, Sussex, Hampshire, Dorset and the several Ports and Watering Places on the Southern Coast from the Mouth of the Thames to the Isle of Portland'. The Petition continued, 'That to these grounds of great local benefit and superior Public convenience Your Petitioners may also ascribe to the projected line somewhat of National Importance from the facility it will afford in case of War for a direct and rapid Transport of Troops from the Garrison of Windsor to some of the largest Military Stations and Dockyards in the Kingdom'.

The stage was now set for the parliamentary battle. The Crown and the Provost and Fellows of Eton (but not the masters!) had given their consent to the Great Western branch line. As the result of negotiations the Crown was prepared to sanction the South Western line from Staines as far as Black Potts — on the Datchet side of the River — with the intention that the South Western Bill and the Windsor Castle and Town Approaches Bill should go forward together. The Provost and Fellows, with some misgivings, appeared to be ready to go along with the Crown. Fears and suspicions were quick, however, to rise to the surface — and, in particular, the Great Western was only too ready to incite the College to oppose the South Western. Charles Saunders wrote to Thomas Batcheldor on 20 November 1846: 'the notice for the South Western Line fixes the terminus for the present Session below Black Potts. There can be no doubt that, if they gain that Bill, they will apply afterwards to extend it either between the College and the Castle or round the College to come into our Windsor Line. Either course must, I conceive, be most seriously prejudicial to the College. We shall be quite ready to give the utmost opposition to it — on behalf both of this Company and the College, if the Provost and Fellows will give every aid and influence to render it effectual'.

The mutual suspicions which prevailed are illustrated by the controversy over the location of the South Western station at Black Potts. Eton had tried to ensure that the station was as far away from College property as possible. The Crown Commissioners had in fact agreed to the station being sited 'one third of a mile lower down the River'. Now, when the detailed plans were published, Eton believed rightly or wrongly that the South Western were trying to move their station nearer to Eton. The company explained that this belief arose from a misunderstanding of the lines of deviation and the need to acquire additional land to provide an approach road to the station from the Slough Road. The College, however, decided to petition against the Bill as a safeguard, at the same time making it clear that they did not wish to jeopardise the Improvements Bill. Feelings ran high. Batcheldor wrote to the Provost on 13 January 1847, 'the contemplated appropriation of the property close to the Shooting Fields and the alteration in the situation of the station and railway terminus are unpardonable departures from the understanding entered into by the College who were clearly led to believe that their property would remain untouched, and they therefore cannot be charged with having acted in a manner not consistent with perfect honour and fairness in this matter for the only breach which has been made has been made by the Railway Company'. These remarks related to a letter written four days before by Col. Reid of the South Western to Lord Morpeth and which the latter had referred to the College for their comments. In it Col. Reid had asked: 'is it consistent with perfect honour and fairness to oppose measures after every point which has been stipulated for has been liberally conceded and every wish had been complied with'? He made reference to 'the full measure of protection which the College has received from the Crown' and ended, 'Permit me again to entreat your Lordship to use your influence both as a Servant of the Crown and as a distinguished Etonian to avert the many evils which the course at present pursued by the College would be certain of producing'. On the 21st, Reid, writing to the Provost, referred to 'the unfair and unfriendly representations of Mr. Batcheldor' and said that his assertions and imputations were 'utterly groundless and unwarrantable'.

The Company gave way, but it was not until April that an Agreement was finally made. Draft after draft went backwards and forwards. The Company wanted to use the word 'Station'; the College tried to insist on 'Terminus'. As late as 1 April the College was still going ahead with its Petition against the Bill and two days later Batcheldor was writing to Drake, the South Western solicitor, criticising the prevarication in signing the

Agreement and saying, 'I hope you will now understand that I will not be driven into a corner in this matter and as the Undertaking has not been sent to Messrs. Tooke (the College solicitors) I beg to say it must be deposited with them on or before Thursday next, or the College will proceed with their opposition'. As the outcome the Bill included the specific statement that the line would 'terminate in the Parish of Datchet in the County of Buckingham in a certain Field distant One thousand one hundred Yards or thereabouts North-west of Datchet Bridge'.

By this time the House of Commons had set up a Committee to examine both the Great Western and the South Western Bills. The Committee did its work speedily and at the beginning of May reached a decision in favour of the South Western. This spelt defeat not only for the Great Western, but also for the Crown and for the Provost and Fellows. Once again 'the Eton masters and the Eton men' had triumphed. Sir Henry Vane, Chairman of the Commons Committee, told Lord Morpeth 'it was exclusively the Eton opposition that threw out the Bill'. Windsor also was pleased. 'The decision of the Parliamentary committee', reported the *Express* on 8 May, 'reached Windsor and Eton by express at half-past 5 o'clock . . . and diffused a general feeling of gratification throughout the two towns'.

At the end of the month the Commissioners announced their decision to postpone the Improvement Bill until the following Session. The announcement was received by the SW directors with dismay, for they realised how much their plans depended on their Agreement with the Crown. Moreover, behind the scenes, the Great Western in anger and frustration that its own Bill had fallen down was still attempting to sabotage the South Western. The *Express* referred to the 'unremitting and unscrupulous exertions of the Great Western directors' with a view to gaining 'the exclusive control and possession of the town and its entire population'.

James Bedborough at this time enjoyed the dual offices of Mayor of Windsor and Director of the Windsor, Staines and South Western Railway Company. He believed, along with the *Express*, that the postponement of the Improvement Bill was due to pressure from the Great Western. Lord Morpeth in fact had written to the SW Directors: 'I find myself in consequence of an Assurance which I gave to the Directors of the Great Western Company unable to proceed with the Windsor Improvement Bill during the present Session'. Bedborough thereupon wrote to Morpeth – in his capacity as Mayor – and received a conciliatory reply, re-assuring him that there was nothing to stop the South Western Bill going ahead on its own. The Bill accordingly went through the remaining stages in the Commons and came before the Lords Committee on 7 June. The Committee sat until the 11th and conducted another of the searching enquiries to which all the Windsor railway projects had to submit.

The chief witness in support of the Bill was Col. George Alexander Reid MP. 'The Town of Windsor', he said, 'has for some time been in a most unthriving cheerless condition, and amongst other causes I attribute its present depression of trade to the want of proper communication with the surrounding districts.' He emphasised the problems of communication with Staines and its neighbourhood in winter. Runnymede was under water for some months of the year. Communication with Staines had therefore to be up Priest Hill and through Englefield Green, a longer route which involved a steep hill in either direction. Problems of access existed for intending visitors to Windsor. 'I believe', said Col. Reid, 'there is scarcely anybody in Great Britain who is not anxious to see Windsor; it is one of the lions of England.' Almost everyone so it seemed – if Col. Reid was to be believed – was in favour of the South Western proposals. At least nine-tenths of Windsor people were in favour of them. Eton College had been fully consulted. So had the Crown. As a result of a deputation to Lord Morpeth, a decision on the location had been left to him, 'including the access into the Town of Windsor across the Park'. The Railway Company 'engaged to pay all the expenses of this arrangement'.

Col Reid, as might be expected from a former officer of the Life Guards, was naturally interested in the use of the railway by the military. When reviews were held at Hounslow, troops marched up from Windsor in the morning and back again in the evening. A railway would enable troops 'to be landed on the ground perfectly fresh and without the fatigue of having walked any distance'. He could not foresee 'the least difficulty in moving a Troop of Cavalry by railway'. Moreover, it would solve the problem of moving baggage and sick. A railway would also be invaluable in cases of disturbances – 'it is of immense advantage to transport troops with great rapidity'.

After Rev. Edward Coleridge of Eton College had expressed the view that the South Western line was much more acceptable to the College than the Great Western, James Bedborough threw all the weight of his long experience, and now of his official position, behind the South Western. He began with a detailed review of earlier projects — probably the most detailed contemporary analysis available to us. Other witnesses included John Secker, George Henry Long, Joseph Locke (engineer-in-chief, SW Railway Co.) and William Tite (architect and surveyor to the South Western). On the other hand some of the local tradesmen were strongly in favour of the Great Western. They maintained that a *central* station in Windsor was required; having a station at Black Potts was no better than having a station at Slough. The whole case for the South Western rested in point of fact on the hope that the railway could be extended from Datchet into Windsor in the near future — and the Crown had not yet consented to this.

Two eminent witnesses were called before the proceedings closed. The first was Sir Robert Peel — though it is not clear why he was called and his evidence is inconclusive. The second was Isambard Kingdom Brunel, Chief Engineer to the Great Western, who expressed the opinion that the traffic between Datchet and Windsor would affect the privacy of the Castle, and that a station at George Street would be much more convenient for Windsor than one at Black Potts.

At this point the Select Committee decided not to hear further witnesses and gave their approval. The Bill then passed through its remaining stages and became law before the end of the month. 'On the intelligence of the royal assent having been given to the Windsor, Staines and South Western Railway Bill being received in Windsor last evening' — so the *Express* reported on 26 June — 'the bells of the parish church were merrily rung in honour of the event.' A Commemoration Ball and Supper at the Town Hall followed on 8 July.

So the South Western had won the first round over the Great Western, although it was not a final victory. Approval had only been given for the construction of the South Western line as far as Datchet, and there was no likelihood that the Great Western would regard its defeat as more than temporary.

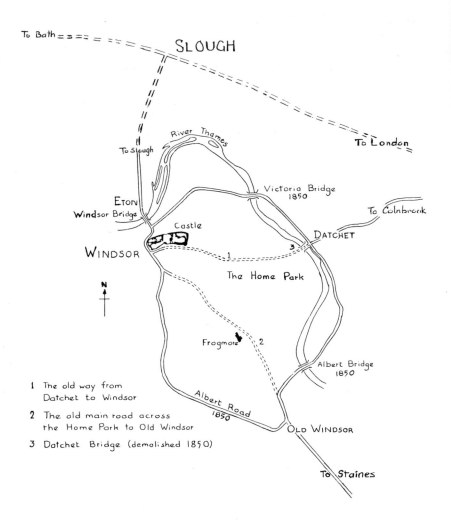

To Bath

SLOUGH

To London

River Thames

To Slough

Victoria Bridge
1850

To Colnbrook

Eton
Windsor Bridge

Castle

DATCHET

WINDSOR

3

1

N

The Home Park

Frogmore

2

Albert Bridge
1850

1 The old way from
Datchet to Windsor

2 The old main road across
the Home Park to Old Windsor

3 Datchet Bridge (demolished 1850)

Albert Road
1850

OLD WINDSOR

To Staines

The 'Improvement Roads'. As the outcome of the bargain between the Crown and the Railway Companies, the ancient ways across the Park to Datchet and Old Windsor were finally superseded by new roads- Windsor to Datchet, Datchet to Old Windsor and Old Windsor to Windsor- in 1850.

Isambard Kingdom Brunel, GWR engineer 1833-59.
Portrait by J.C. Horsley. (NPG)

70

ABOVE: 'Perfectly unique in all its contrivances.' Two views of Brunel's single-span Great Western railway Bridge, 1849. (RES) LEFT: Joseph Locke, engineer to the Windsor, Staines and South Western Railway. Portrait by Sir Francis Grant. (ICE)

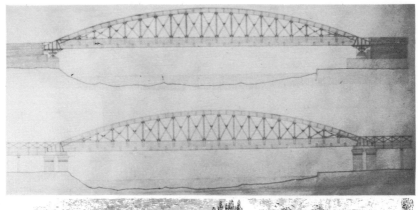

ABOVE: Drawings of Brunel's Bridge-
after and before the partial reconstruction of the abutments at the beginning
of the present century. The lower drawing shows the original bridge with its
tubular columns and open viaduct.
CENTRE: Richmond Bridge, one of
Locke's two bridges over the Thames on
the South Western line from London to
Windsor. (ILN) BELOW LEFT: Col.
Alexander Reid, MP for Windsor 1845-

52. Prominent in the railway negoti-
ations, especially as a champion of the
South Western. (ILN) RIGHT: Henry
Darvill, Windsor solicitor, Mayor and
later Town Clerk. Local solicitor first
for the Windsor, Slough and Staines
Atmospheric Railway and later for the
GWR.

THE CROWN YIELDS — AT A PRICE

No railway could approach or enter Windsor without the sanction of the Crown. Any railway promoter who tried to ignore this fact was doomed — as the Windsor, Slough and Staines Atmospheric Railway Company found to its cost. Both the Home Park and the Great Park seemed to impose an insuperable physical barrier to the approach of any railway from London direct into Windsor. But the Crown's control was not limited to the Park. Any attempt to *sneak* into Windsor by way of Romney Island or the towpath had no chance of success. In fact until at least 1845 the Crown was not prepared to sanction any approach to Windsor. Charles Saunders told a parliamentary enquiry: 'We endeavoured to ascertain how far it would be consistent with the wishes of the Court that any line should come into Windsor and we were told that they were desirous that no line whatever should be promoted'. The Earl of Lincoln, Chief Commissioner under Peel, recollected in 1848 that 'there was a great indisposition to have any Railway approaching Windsor nearer than the Great Western at Slough'.

The one exception seems to be the early episode of William IV granting his consent to a railway across the Park. But, even leaving on one side the question about what sort of railway it was, the project was still-born and there is no evidence that this precedent influenced the attitude of the Crown in the 1840s.

Prince Albert, with his interest in scientific and industrial developments, was clearly alive to the possibilities of railways. As we have seen, he made his first railway journey — from Slough to Paddington — on 14 November 1839 and, after his marriage to Queen Victoria in February 1840, frequently travelled by train. Victoria has an entry in her Journal for 8 February 1837 — four months before she became Queen: 'We went to see the Railroad near Hersham, and saw the steam carriage pass with surprising quickness, striking sparks as it flew along the railroad, enveloped in clouds of smoke and making a loud noise. It is a very curious thing indeed'. She did not make her first actual train journey until 13 June 1842 when she travelled from Slough to Paddington with the Prince and their suite. From this time she also travelled regularly by train.

Too much importance need not perhaps be attached to the stories that Prince Albert thought the vibrations from the trains would cause the Castle to collapse or that the Queen objected to the smoke polluting the area and dirtying her clean castle walls. The railway none the less did pose a threat. At vast expense, the Castle, between 1824 and 1836, had been transformed into what was almost a new building, magnificent, spectacular, a fitting setting for the Court which from now on made it the chief royal residence of the country. Almost at this precise moment, the steam locomotive arrived on the scene and all over the country began to oust the coaches with their smart equipages, and the new locomotive was noisy *and* dirty. A correspondent to the *Windsor Express* in November 1844 asked how a railway could be brought into the town 'without destroying the scenery from the Castle, and encroaching upon its privacy as a monarchical residence'? Moreover, by this time — even though the railway as yet approached no nearer than Slough — the influx of visitors to Windsor was increasing. As early as 1834 a correspondent to the *Berkshire Chronicle* prophesied that the railway would bring to Windsor 'to behold the seat of Royalty, all the ladies of St. Giles and the Seven Dials, with the gentlemen their paramours, and others of the same grade from Old Drury, Field Lane, Billingsgate, Rag Fair etc . . . ' In 1847 Col. Phipps, Private Secretary to Prince Albert, confided to Lord Morpeth, the Chief Commissioner, that he thought that 'a station upon or near the site of the brewery', where the South Western Station was to be two years later, 'would I think be highly objectionable. The shortest way, to and from it, would be by the "Hundred Steps" and would pour the whole tide of the lowest class — the foot passengers — in flux and reflux thro' the Castle'.

In spite of all the forebodings the railways did come to Royal Windsor. The Great Western and the South Western came within a few yards of the Castle and the South Western line came into Windsor across the Home Park. Even, however, when the Crown yielded and accepted in principle that a railway must come into Windsor from Staines, it was 'implacably opposed to a line approaching from Old Windsor', that is, to any intrusion into the Park to the south of the Castle.

After the failure of the projects in the 1830s, there was something of a lull for several years. 'The projects', said James Bedborough, 'all slept until 1844.' On 12 October of that year the notices first appeared of the proposed Windsor Junction Railway. About the same time the Great Western Railway Company revived its plans for a branch line from Slough to Windsor. The Prince, no doubt well informed, immediately got in touch with the Prime Minister and Sir Robert Peel wrote on 15 October: 'Sir, The Board of Trade has received no information respecting the project of a Rail Road from Slough to Windsor. There is a project of one from Windsor to London passing near Staines and Putney — to the south side of Waterloo Bridge.

'I would recommend Your Royal Highness to take no step whatever at present with respect to the proposed Railway from Slough to Windsor, to decline expressing any opinion respecting it and to reserve an unfettered power of action when any *serious* proposal shall be made.

'It does not appear to me to be politic to *encourage* a Railway between Slough and Windsor — and if it is not the best plan is to remain entirely passive. Inquiries at present — or the attempt to judge of comparative merits of Rival Schemes would be construed into approbation of the principle of a Railway from Slough to Windsor. [Signed] Robert Peel.'

The Prince acknowledged Peel's letter, replying 'I shall follow your advice with respect to the proposed Railway'. This brief but significant correspondence helps to explain the Prince's apparent silence in the railway controversies of the next few years. There is, however, no question that the Queen and the Prince maintained a close watch on all local railway proposals and developments. There are many scarcely veiled allusions to their interest. Thus Col. Phipps wrote at the end of a long letter to Lord Morpeth in 1847: 'I cannot but feel that you may think me presumptuous in stating all this as *my* opinion, but I think you know me well enough to believe I would not have taken the liberty to do so, without being certain that I was borne out in my views by the opinions of those most worthy of attention'. In addition witnesses at the parliamentary enquiries occasionally let slip some fragment of information. Thomas Page, engineer for the 1844 project, said that the plans had been laid before the Queen in person. Peel divulged that at the time of the Corn Law crisis he had discussed local railway proposals with the Queen at Windsor. Saunders said that Morpeth had told him that the Queen would never give her consent to a railway line between the Castle and the River – and one can almost hear the Queen saying it.

The personal involvement of the Queen and the Prince is largely hidden behind the facade of the Commissioners of Woods and Forests. They constituted in effect a Government department, with a head who was a minister and often a member of the Cabinet. Their responsibilities from 1832 to 1851 covered not only the management of Crown lands but public buildings including embassies overseas. In 1851 there was a separation of functions and the Works department was given the parliamentary head (later represented by the Minister of Works) and the Office of Woods and Forests was left in charge of two commissioners, both of them officials.

Thus, during the 1840s, the Chief Commissioners were Government ministers, holding important and responsible positions. They dealt with Crown estates in almost every English county, as well as in Scotland, Ireland and Wales, and with works in embassies in Paris and Constantinople. Locally, they concerned themselves with what seemed even the most trifling details affecting the Castle, the Great Park, the Home Park, the Forest, negotiations with the Windsor Corporation – and of course the Windsor railways. The three Chief Commissioners who cover almost the whole of the 1840s are the Earl of Lincoln (Chief Commissioner in Peel's Conservative administration of 1841-46), Charles Canning (Feb – July 1846) and Viscount Morpeth (Chief Commissioner in Lord John Russell's Whig Government from July 1846). All three had been to Eton and to Christ Church, Oxford, before entering politics.

Canning, much better known as Governor-General of India at the time of the Mutiny, served as Chief Commissioner for too short a period to make an impact on the Windsor railway scene. Lincoln and Morpeth, however, were deeply involved both in local negotiations and in the parliamentary enquiries. Both were aristocrats – Lincoln became Duke of Newcastle in 1851 and Morpeth Earl of Carlisle in 1848. Lincoln, friend of Gladstone (who also was at Eton and Christ Church, Oxford!), had been in Parliament since 1832 and was First Commissioner of Woods and Forests for almost the whole of the five years of

Peel's Government, becoming a member of the Cabinet in 1845. He followed Gladstone in supporting Peel over the Corn Law issue and, like so many of the Peelites, suffered the consequences by spending several years in the political wilderness — although his help was enlisted in the thankless task of trying to reconcile the Great Western and the South Western over the Windsor railway conflict. Later, under Aberdeen and Palmerston, he was Colonial Secretary, and for a brief and unfortunate period at the beginning of the Crimean War in charge of the War Office.

Morpeth, nearly ten years older than Lincoln — he was born in 1802 — entered the House of Commons as a Whig in 1826 and gave evidence of his liberal leanings by supporting Catholic and Jewish relief as well as parliamentary reform. He was Chief Secretary for Ireland from 1835 to 1841 — which should have been a useful apprenticeship for the tough assignment in 1846 when, as Russell's Chief Commissioner for Woods and Forests, he inherited the problem of the Windsor Railways. From 1846 to 1848 he represented the West Riding of Yorkshire, with Richard Cobden as his colleague, before he succeeded his father as Earl of Carlisle. 1848 was a crucial year also in another of Morpeth's fields of responsibility — that of public health. Lincoln had prepared a Public Health Bill in 1845; crowded out in 1846, this was revived with various changes in 1847 and again in 1848 and Morpeth had the task of piloting the Bill through Parliament. Later he returned to Irish affairs and was Lord-Lieutenant of Ireland for some eight years before his death in 1864. It has been written of him that he 'was able and kind-hearted, with cultivated tastes and great fluency of speech. Without commanding abilities or great strength of will, his gentleness endeared him to all those with whom he came into contact'. Harriet Martineau called him 'the best and most beloved man in the company of statesmen of his day and generation'. His conscientiousness and sincerity certainly find expression in his letters, with their neat handwriting, orderly arrangement and human understanding.

These were some of the men who were responsible for the railway negotiations carried on in the name of the Crown. Attempts to approach the Queen or the Prince directly were always repelled. Thus, when Charles Saunders, worried about further threats to the Great Western Bill despite the approval of the Commissioners, wrote to Phipps on 22 May 1848, 'I am quite confident that Her Majesty and His Royal'Highness will not permit any obstacle to be thrown in our way after all that has passed', Phipps declined to involve the Crown and replied, 'The proper organ of the expression of the wishes of the Crown is the Office of Woods and the only one that can be properly quoted. My natural course would be to send your Letter to Lord Morpeth for his consideration'.

As we have seen, the first proposals to be brought forward after the failures of the 1830s were the Atmospheric projects of 1844–46. The promoters were optimistic because they believed that they had found the answer to the objections which the Court quite naturally had to the noise and smoke of the steam locomotive. The approach to Windsor from Staines still raised the same problems, that it must be across the Park — until in 1845 the promoters of the Windsor, Slough and Staines Atmospheric Railway believed that by using the Romney Island route they could avoid coming across Crown property at all. The Crown, however, offered no encouragement or support and one after another of the projects met with defeat.

In the meantime the Great Western was watching and waiting. The project of a branch line from Slough to Windsor had indeed certain advantages from the Crown's point of view. It had been longest in the field. Most important, it did not need to cross the Park to come into Windsor. Clearly, discussions were proceeding behind the scenes and on 15 February 1846 Peel wrote to the Queen: 'Sir Robert Peel saw Mr. Saunders the Secretary to the Great Western Railway yesterday and recommended him to take measures for procuring the assent of Eton College to a Line of Railway from Slough to Windsor to be undertaken by the Great Western and for opposing the Lines at present before Parliament. Mr. Saunders is in communication with Mr. Page'.

This reflects a definite change from the tone of Peel's letter to the Prince of October 1844. Over the next few months, however, the Corn Law crisis was raging and the Atmospheric Bill was not rejected until 19 May.

When Peel's Government fell on 29 June 1846, no progress had been made in promoting further Windsor railway projects. With the rejection of the Atmospheric Bill, a position of stalemate seemed to have returned. Yet within a few months the Crown had consented to the construction not only of the Great Western branch line, but of a South Western line from Staines as far as Datchet.

How had the change of heart come about? One reason was undoubtedly the constant pressure of the railway companies. Another was the obvious desire of the people of Windsor for railway communications, especially with London, and it is clear that the change of Government paved the way for a more positive approach. Lincoln had been cautious in the extreme. Morpeth was anxious to find a solution and was prepared to negotiate with both the Great Western and South Western.

The decisive factor, however, was the Crown's need for money to finance improvements in the surroundings of the Castle. The Castle itself had been transformed. It was naturally felt that the transformation was incomplete without the improvement also of the environment. There seemed two main obstacles. One was the existence of the squalid houses that lined the Castle ditch in Thames Street, High Street, Castle Hill and its neighbourhood. The second arose from the inconvenience — to the Castle — of the public ways that traversed the Park.

The cost of the reconstruction of the Castle had caused a public outcry. Undoubtedly this was a reason why the Crown was reluctant to approach Parliament for money for the further improvements now contemplated.

The needs of the railway companies were the Crown's opportunity. Step by step the Crown appeared to yield — but it secured £85,000 from the railway companies in the process and was able to carry through in their entirety the grandiose schemes of new roads, new bridges, improvements in the setting of the Castle that were embodied in the 'Windsor Castle and Town Approaches Act', finally passed in 1848.

The surrender — if such it can be called — was spread over at least two years. Peel's letter to the Queen in February 1846 shows that the principle of a Great Western branch from Slough to Windsor had at last been accepted by the Crown. We have seen how, after the rejection of the Atmospheric Bill, public opinion in Windsor swung round in favour of the South Western project of a line from Staines. The Crown moved cautiously towards a qualified support for the South Western. Negotiations with the Great Western, however, proceeded rapidly. Morpeth wrote to Anson, Phipps' predecessor as Secretary to Prince Albert, on 5 November 1846: 'The Great Western pressed their independent Line, and I thought they could not be refused.

We are binding the Great Western to as much of the specified conditions as can be comprised in their Act of Parliament; anything beyond we shall probably have to provide for in a special Act we must bring in for stopping up some of the roads'.

The controversy over the location of the Black Potts Station has already been described. It is clear that the main points of the Agreement between the Commissioners and the South Western had been settled by November 1846, following the meetings in October. Drake, the South Western solicitor, mentions in a letter to Morpeth that it was on 3 November that it had been agreed that the precise location of the Station should be fixed by the Commissioners. The suspicions of Eton delayed the final Agreement until 10 May 1847. By this the South Western Company committed itself to making a payment of £60,000 to the Crown.

The intention was that the South Western Bill, the Great Western Bill and the Improvements Bill should all go forward together. Then came the rejection of the Great Western Bill in May 1847. There is no doubt that this represented a setback for the Crown. Morpeth's letters show considerable concern and considerable doubt about the best way forward. He realised that there was no question of going back on the Crown's promises to the Great Western. 'I can only add', he wrote at the end of a letter to Col. Phipps immediately after the rejection, 'that I should be ready to take any step in my power to facilitate the passing of their Branch in another Session'. A further letter on the following day (16 May 1847) illustrates his complete uncertainty about the course to take and a third on the 18th said: 'Under present circumstances, I think the Great Western will be satisfied if we do not press the Windsor Improvement Bill this Session. I think to avoid unpleasant discussion this had better be acquiesced in; it would now come on under unfavourable circumstances, and no great difference would take place in ultimately effecting it. It would be more convenient too with respect to money. But the great point is to get out of the present heats as smoothly as we can. Will you let me know as soon as you can whether the giving up of the Bill for this Session would be sanctioned'. In a postscript he added, 'We cannot in any way stop the South Western, and it will be for the best that their Bill should pass'. These three letters in four days were all to Col. Phipps and were obviously intended to receive the consideration of the Prince and the Queen. In the event the decision was taken to hold up the Improvements

Bill until the following Session. Both the South Western and the Windsor Corporation (which was anxious to see the demolition of the remaining houses in the Castle Ditch and had given the Bill its full support) received the news with manifest regret.

It was not until October 1847 that further meetings took place between the Commissioners and the representatives of the Railway Companies — with the Great Western on the 25th and the South Western on the 26th. Morpeth was obviously worried by the antagonism between the two — in a letter to Phipps on the 29th he commented, 'You may have seen in the papers that I am already beset by both the Great & South Western, so the troubles of the campaign are already begun'. The Great Western wanted the fullest possible support from the Crown in their effort 'to mollify the Eton opposition'. Phipps, who was not quite as much in the thick of the fight as Morpeth and therefore was able to take a more detached view, said of the Great Western, 'They have undoubtedly like the hero of the Nursery Rhyme "had a great fall", but they must become also thoroughly convinced that all the King's men cannot place Humpty Dumpty as he was again . . .' On the other hand, as Morpeth said, 'the South Western are jealous of the notion of the Gr Wn getting into the town of Windsor, when they will be stopped at Black Potts & make suggestions for being allowed to carry on their rail-line further. I told them this could not be heard of'.

A new Agreement was made between the Commissioners and the Great Western, as a result of which the Crown pledged itself to approve the construction of the branch line into the centre of the town in return for the payment of £25,000.

Morpeth, asked why the Crown had decided to support the Great Western Bill, answered: 'Because the passage of the Great Western Bill, according to an agreement which has been entered into between the Office of Woods and the Great Western Company, would put the Office of Woods in possession of the Funds which would be necessary to effect the improvements contemplated under the Windsor Improvement Bill'. The Directors of the Great Western and officials such as Charles Saunders obviously considered that the Crown had done well out of the transaction. It had secured — at no expense to itself — a line and station admirably sited to serve the Court. It had exacted a contribution of £25,000 towards the Windsor Improvements.

It had ensured the demolition of George Street and its unsavoury neighbourhood in close proximity to the Castle. It had imposed a whole series of restrictions to safeguard the amenities of the Castle — there was, for example, to be 'no manufacturing or repairing of Steam or other Engines or Carriages'. And it had obtained a pledge that the Company would erect 'a handsome and commodious Station' and, among other buildings, 'accommodation for the personal use, privacy and comfort of Her Majesty'. One proposal which never materialised was a bridge over Thames Street from the Station to the Castle to provide a private way for the Queen.

Similarly, a new Agreement, dated 2 November 1847, was entered into with the South Western. It provided for the payment of the £60,000 in instalments of £10,000. Assuming that Black Potts would remain the terminus, it required: that there should be no making of coke or repairs to engines and railway stock at the station; that the station and buildings should not occupy more than five acres; that any buildings should be subject to the consent in writing of the Commissioners; that no beer shop should be opened nor should there be any other business or use which might constitute a nuisance; and that no application for an extension of the Line should be made without the consent in writing of the Commissioners.

A clause of the Agreement which was to have repercussions over a century later was that which provided that the bridge and the road from Datchet to Windsor should be 'for ever thereafter kept in complete and sufficient repair by the said Company in such manner as the said Commissioners for the time being should direct'. In 1963 the bridge in question — the Victoria Bridge — was found to be unsafe and British Rail was surprised and not a little disconcerted to find it was under a legal obligation to repair it.

So in November 1847 the way was clear for the Improvements Bill and the second Great Western Bill to be introduced into Parliament.

There was one dilemma which the Crown never resolved. Lincoln told a parliamentary enquiry in 1848, 'certainly it has always been my opinion that if more than one Company were to enter Windsor, it would be most desirable that they should enter at the same spot'. Gladstone said that two stations would be 'a very decided evil to a Town of that Nature'. The antagonism between the two companies in any case made it almost impossible to secure co-operation between them. Robert Stephenson said, 'there can be no doubt that if the two companies had no rivalry between them but were merely considering the public convenience they would ultimately bring the two stations together. The separation is attributable entirely to the rivalry between the parties'. The Crown, moreover, was fundamentally opposed to the one line of approach to Windsor which would have achieved its objective, namely, that across the Home Park. Time and again the Commissioners, like nineteenth century Canutes, said that they did not want the railway to come nearer than Black Potts. Yet, if a line was constructed joining Slough and Black Potts, its continuation into Windsor could only be a matter of time and there was no other practicable route into Windsor from Black Potts but one that would cross the Home Park.

Most of the projects for the single entrance into Windsor assume a link between the South Western and the Great Western *east* of Eton. This would presumably have ruled out the need for the Great Western branch line from Slough to Windsor – which was of course a reason why all such projects were opposed, either openly or clandestinely, by the Great Western. One interesting proposal with a difference – because it accepted the Great Western branch line – is contained in a pamphlet written by 'R.R.T.', dated 1 January 1847 and printed for private circulation. 'R.R.T.' was R.R. Tighe, a leading figure in some of the railway projects of the 1840s – he was, for example, Secretary of the Windsor Junction Company.

A copy of his eleven page pamphlet is filed in the Royal Archives at Windsor and it is interesting to speculate that Morpeth, Phipps and perhaps the Prince himself gave its proposals serious consideration. Tighe emphasises the limitations of a South Western railway to Black Potts by itself and a Great Western branch line by itself. He suggests that the South Western line from Staines should proceed to the north of Datchet to Slough, linking with the Great Western Slough to Windsor branch line, with provision for both gauges. The branch line should run close in to Eton and 'cross the river a little above the Eyot, so much used for the pleasure boats and fireworks. The bridge, for which two arches with one pier would suffice, would act as a breakwater, improving and preserving the little island, which, without some small protection, will be soon carried away'. Tighe was anxious to assuage the possible apprehensions of both the College and the Crown. The railway would be on 'elevated railways'. It would be well-fenced throughout, and any possible intrusion (by Eton scholars) might be prevented by a parapet fence of open iron works, sufficiently high to protect the railway passengers from anything thrown at the carriages. Tighe obviously took at their face value the comments that Carter, Hawtrey and others made about 'the nature of Eton boys', but he added, 'it is an ill-compliment, however, to Etonians to suppose that they would be guilty of such an offence'. He had two suggestions for eliminating noise. 'The whistle', he said, 'might be easily dispensed with by the more frequent use of the Electric Telegraph, announcing the departure and arrival of every train'. And — in a footnote — 'the reported success of Mr. Brunel's experiments on the South Devon line, with the principle of Atmospheric traction, suggests its application to the proposed lines between Slough and Windsor, thus dispensing with the locomotive engine.' This line, concluded Tighe, would afford all the combined advantages of the Great Western and the South Western.

Tighe's proposals may have been sincere and carefully thought out, but, in the whirl of conflicting interests and attitudes of College, Castle, the Great Western and South Western, they had little chance of success.

The Commissioners continued, however, to explore the possibilities of avoiding the need for two lines and two stations. One section of the Agreement between the Crown and the South Western (10 May 1847) provided for a Great Western branch from Slough to link with the South Western terminus at Black Potts. Discussions, perhaps increasingly spasmodic, continued throughout 1847 and into 1848. Neither the Great Western nor the College wanted a line to the east of Eton, but felt it impolitic to go against the Crown. Brunel expressed the opinion that 'a line coming out of the Great Western at a point east of Slough Station' and linking with Black Potts was not practicable. This would, he said, have been a convenience for the South Western 'with a view of communication westward', but not the Great Western. The latter clung to its own branch line like a limpet; it did not want to co-operate with the South Western and was quite prepared to play upon Eton's fears. The nearest the College came to giving its approval was when it told the Great Western that 'if a Line could be made from Slough to Windsor in conjunction with the SW Railway Line but so as not to have any station, waiting place etc on the line they are willing to allow a line to cross Black Potts but not otherwise'. Bethell, the College Bursar, however, wrote to the Provost, who was at Brighton, with reference to the proposed Slough to Black Potts line, 'any approach nearer to the Playing Fields and the adjoining property of the College They cannot consent to'.

The Crown really gave up the hope of avoiding the two lines when it committed itself to supporting the GW Branch Line — and this, as we have seen, goes back to the early part of 1846. Morpeth, seeking to allay the fears of the Great Western as late as May 1848, wrote to Saunders, 'The proposed line of the Great Western to George Street has received the full approval of the Crown'. The South Western at this stage tried to promote its own line from Black Potts to Slough, and introduced a Bill (The Windsor, Staines and South Western Bill. Slough Extension and Deviations and Slough Extension to Windsor) into Parliament. It met with opposition both from the Crown and from the Great Western and on 2 June 1848 the parliamentary committee in rejecting it expressed the opinion that 'a communication between Windsor and Slough would be better provided for by another bill which the committee have had under their consideration' — the Great Western Branch Bill.

Gradually, in 1848, the Crown seems to have become reconciled to the extension of the South Western line across the Home Park into Windsor. Whatever the theoretical advantages of the joint line, the practical difficulties were too great. Even the problems of the different gauges were very real. An approach line to Windsor, providing for both the broad and the narrow gauge, would, as Morpeth said, have been 'a multiplication of the inconvenience'. As late as May 1848, however, Morpeth told Saunders, 'It was clearly stipulated that the promoters of the South Western line should not extend it over the River into Windsor. The Crown has not given its consent to such a line'. Yet by August the announcement was made at the half-yearly meeting of the South Western Company that 'Her Majesty had graciously consented to an extension of the Windsor, Staines and South Western line from Datchet across the Home Park into Windsor'.

When the final Agreement was made between the Crown and the South Western on 14 February 1849, the extension into Windsor was already — with the approval of the Crown — under construction.

ABOVE LEFT: A fanciful representation of the Royal Family leaving Windsor by rail. RIGHT: Viscount Morpeth, later Earl of Carlisle. (Viscount Morpeth) Portrait by John Partridge. BELOW LEFT: The Earl of Lincoln, later Duke of Newcastle.(NPG) RIGHT: Royal Waiting Room and Station adjoining the South Western Station. (RES)

Royal Waiting Room at the Great Western Station at Windsor. This belongs to a later period in Victoria's reign, but illustrates the luxurious accommodation which the railway companies sought to provide for royalty.

ETON GOES DOWN FIGHTING

Eton was dominated by the College as Windsor was dominated by the Castle. In 1833 — when the Great Western Company first put forward its railway proposals — the College contained 570 boys. The numbers fluctuated considerably as the reputation of the College rose and fell, but Eton's position as England's premier school was already well-established. Many of the sons of the aristocracy and gentry passed through the College and received there, against a background of rowdiness and indiscipline, the traditional classical education. Lytton Strachey referred to 'a life in which licensed barbarism was mingled with the daily and hourly study of the niceties of Ovidian verse'. Even within the confines of the traditional education there had been little change. The Eton Latin grammar in use in the 1830s was virtually the same as that in use in the sixteenth century.

The 'licensed barbarism' to which Lytton Strachey referred is illustrated by a hundred different stories — of the tyranny of the seniors, the servitude of the juniors, the horrors and orgies of Long Chamber where the Collegers were locked in for ten or eleven hours without supervision every night, poaching expeditions in Windsor Park, escapades at Windsor Fair or Windsor races . . . And what can be said when the headmaster himself *expected* the boys to fight the navvies or to throw stones at passing trains? Even royalty did not escape. Arthur Coleridge, in his *Eton in the Forties*, described 'the traditionary practice of bawling at the royal carriage'. 'Our boisterous loyalty', he wrote, 'must have tried the young Queen's nerves, though they had plenty of practice, for she and her Ministers repeatedly drove through Eton to the Castle, and it was our custom to run alongside the royal carriage, as near as the cavalry escort would allow us, and hurl our stormy cheers in her face'.

Yet many of these boys grew up to become respected leaders in the public life of nineteenth century England. True, some, like Robert Cecil, later as Lord Salisbury, Foreign Secretary and

Prime Minister, hated the recollection of their days at Eton. Many, however, looking back on their school days with nostalgia, were opposed to any change that threatened Eton's traditional way of life.

When the railway story began, Dr. Keate, headmaster, and Dr. Goodall, Provost, were still at Eton. Keate, short and stocky, with bull-dog face and red bushy eyebrows beneath his huge cocked hat, and Goodall, with knee-breeches and powdered wig, were eighteenth century men struggling, uncomprehending, against the tides of the nineteenth century. The stories of the victimisation of Keate by generations of his young barbarians and his retaliatory floggings are enshrined in the legends of Eton. Keate retired in 1834 to become a Canon of Windsor; Goodall, the arch-conservative, remained Provost until 1840. Their departures paved the way for change, though certainly not revolutionary change.

'But times are changed, and we are changed,
And Keate has passed away.'

The portraits of the men who ruled Eton are sketched from personal recollection in Arthur Coleridge's book — Thomas Carter, Bursar, Fellow, father of Canon Carter who brought the Oxford Movement to Clewer where he was Rector from 1844 to 1880; George Bethell, Carter's successor as Bursar, renowned for his strident voice; Edward Coleridge, Senior Assistant Master, implacable enemy of the railways; Richard Okes, Lower Master; William Gifford Cookesley, Assistant Master. All were in Holy Orders; all, as boy and man, had passed the greater part of their lives at Eton; all were involved in the railway controversies and appeared at the parliamentary enquiries.

It was Dr. Edward Hawtrey, however, headmaster from 1834 to 1852, who was foremost in the confrontation between Eton and the railway companies. He appeared in person at every one of the parliamentary enquiries of the 1840s, when the interests of Eton were at stake. In the general history of the College he occupies an important place. Maxwell Lyte, the historian of Eton, said of him, 'Hawtrey may be said to have done by encouraging what Keate tried to do by threatening'. He was not afraid to introduce changes. In 1846, for example, he got rid of Long Chamber, with its traditions of bullying and with its lack of elementary sanitary and washing amenities. The foundation stone of the new buildings along the east side of Weston's Yard was laid by Prince Albert in 1844 and the buildings were opened two years later. But on the railway issue Hawtrey never yielded an inch. His answers during periods of cross-examination at the enquiries were completely uncompromising; in his view railways threatened all that Eton stood for and he would oppose them, if necessary, even against the Crown and even against the governing body of the College itself. Linguist, conversationalist, bibliophile, above all an Etonian, his personality emerges sharply. Arthur Coleridge, who was at Eton under Hawtrey, wrote: 'He was so delightfully *rococo*, one of his assistants said, and certainly his pineapple-shaped head, his curiously grotesque face and action, combined with his fine-gentleman ways, made a very strange ensemble'.

Thomas Batcheldor is another who has a place of special importance in the railway controversies. As College Registrar from 1827 to his death in 1866 he was responsible for many of the negotiations with the railway companies, for preparing the presentation of the College case at the enquiries, for drafts of 'safeguarding clauses' and petitions. He was simultaneously in the employment of the Dean and Canons of St. George's, first as Clerk of the Lands and then, from 1843, as Chapter Clerk. Nicknamed 'Hoppy' because of his one short leg, he was a familiar figure at Eton for many years. His passion was fishing and he was an angler in the Izaac Walton tradition. He leased from the College and from the Windsor Corporation various eyots in the Thames – one was Black Potts; another, upstream, is described as 'Batcheldor's Eyot'. The Atmospheric railway would have passed across the eyots. The South Western eventually crossed the river near Batcheldor's house, and it adds a certain poignancy to the story of his negotiations that over and above his official interest his personal interests were deeply involved.

Such was Eton in the thirties and forties. Into this environment, with its remoteness from the industrialism and the radicalism which were beginning to transform the country, came the railways. It is difficult to imagine a more revolutionary and more unwelcome intrusion. To come to terms with the railway age was not easy for Eton; it could only take place by a slow and often agonising process of adjustment. The position of the College was in many respects an unenviable one. At various times Eton had to face the prospect of being completely boxed in – railways to the north, railways to the west, railways to the east, railways to the south. In point of fact, when the pattern was finally settled, Eton had railways on three sides out of the four.

We have seen that Eton's response to the first plans in 1833-35 was unyielding. It is difficult sometimes to assess the relative responsibility of the College and the Crown for the defeat of successive railway proposals. But Eton at least was vocal in its opposition. It opposed the still-born London and Windsor Railway. It successfully opposed the Slough to Windsor branch line proposal. With less success it opposed the Great Western main line, but at least when the Bill became law in 1835 the College was able to secure the prohibition of any station or future railway line within three miles. As a direct consequence of this, although the College lost the battle to prevent the Great Western from picking up or setting down passengers at Slough, it did for a time prevent the construction of a station.

Eton, however, came — especially in the later years — to speak with two voices in the railway controversy. The Eton masters, with one or two exceptions, maintained their opposition to the bitter end — and they received a great deal of support from many Etonians in positions of influence. But the governing body of the College consisted of the Provost and Fellows, not the masters, and although they exacted their pound of flesh from the railway companies in the shape of numerous safeguards, they were prepared, especially with the two great Companies, to negotiate rather than meet every proposal with inflexible opposition.

Provost Goodall was said to have been willing to give consent to a railway — presumably a branch line from Slough to Windsor — as early as 1836. Negotiations came to the point of agreement in 1839, but the proposed bill never went into Parliament — most likely as the result of the dissent of the Crown.

When, however, there were new proposals in 1844-46, Eton again closed its ranks. The veto of the Crown was sufficient to kill the Windsor Junction Railway, though, as we have seen, Dr. Hawtrey left nothing to chance and attended the initial meeting to watch over the interests of the College. The Windsor, Slough and Staines Atmospheric Railway Company, however, represented a greater threat, because it received powerful local support and introduced its Bill into Parliament. Moreover, since by using the Romney Island route the railway did not pass over Crown land, the Crown kept in the background. The first action of Eton was to purchase Romney Island from the Thames Commissioners as a safeguard against the railway. A Statement of the College Case was drawn up and circulated. A Petition was adopted and forwarded to Parliament. And, when the parliamentary enquiry took place, Eton engaged Counsel and successfully deployed all its formidable resources in opposition to the Bill.

The Atmospheric railway would have involved lines both to the south of Eton — along Romney Island — and to the east, coming close in to the College. The South Western and Great Western proposals which emerged later in 1846 threatened lines to the south and the west of Eton — and there was also the proposal of a line to the east of Eton linking the Great Western at Slough with the South Western at Black Potts. None the less the Provost and Fellows at this stage were prepared to negotiate and to compromise. There was a growing acceptance of the probability that the railways would have to come and, moreover, a genuine desire to keep in line with the Crown — and negotiated settlements with the railway companies were now becoming the policy of the Crown. The relationship between the College and the South Western passed through a difficult phase as the result of the suspicions which the College entertained of the Company's alleged prevarication in the siting of the Black Potts station, and the College persisted in its Petition against the Bill until it was satisfied. The negotiations with the Great Western proceeded without any major hitch — with an anxious company trying to hurry up a dilatory College. Thus, on 14 October 1846 Saunders sent a plan prepared by Brunel of a new route recommended 'as affording the best accommodation to Eton and Windsor'. Meetings between the company and the College were held on 15 and 27 October and at the second meeting the Provost and Fellows gave their consent to the route proposed. Saunders had, however, to write at least four times to request the sealed agreement. He got it eventually and the Company's 'Receipt of the Consent of the College to the Windsor Railway, subject to the conditions specified' is in the College Records — but undated. The Great Western Bill, which had been deposited in November, was now in a position to proceed.

The Company failed, however, to take account of the strength of the Eton opposition. The masters mobilised the opposition to the Bill from the time it was first proposed and, when in May 1847 it eventually came before the Commons Select Committee, it was rejected. This was the high-water mark of the power of 'the Eton masters and the Eton men'. The Crown had approved the Great Western Bill. The Provost and Fellows had approved. But the Eton opposition was strong enough to prevail not only over the powerful Great Western lobby in Parliament, but over the governing body of their own College, even over the Crown itself.

Morpeth went to see Hawtrey on 16 May, after the rejection of the Bill, and reported to Phipps, 'I find the Eton feeling so strong, and the agitation so organised, that I feel confident no difference of phrase I could have used in my evidence would have had the effect of in the least influencing the decision of the Committee'. Efforts to find a way out of the impasse failed and Morpeth again had to report to Phipps: 'Eton is immovable'.

The Crown could not opt out of the controversy. The passing of the Windsor Improvements Bill, to which it was now committed, was dependent upon the passing of the Great Western Bill as well as the South Western. So, when a second Great Western Bill was promoted in the autumn of 1847, Morpeth made every effort to gain Eton's acquiescence. He sent Lord Barrington and John Talbot to Eton with a letter for Dr. Hawtrey, but had to report to Phipps that they 'met with very little success. Mr. Coleridge is furiously vehement against them and Dr. H will not be brought to believe that there is any real feeling on the top of the Hill in their favour. If there was any opportunity of conveying the impression that the Great Western has really the good wishes of the Castle, it might rather assist matters. I have already said as much on the subject as I can with propriety'.

In his reply Phipps remarked: 'It would be advisable to ascertain, if possible, whether the opposition of Mr. Coleridge, and the other authorities of Eton would be likely to be mitigated were it ascertained by them that the inclination here was favourable to the passing of the GW Bill and should Mr. Coleridge still be implacable whether his opposition would necessarily carry with it such unanimity and strength in the College Authorities as to necessitate the defeat of the Bill'.

Hawtrey himself wrote to Morpeth, saying that he was still unchanged in his opinions, but at the same time wished to make it clear that he was not guilty of any disloyalty to the

Crown. The views of the Crown had obviously been conveyed to Dr. Hawtrey, but he was still not prepared to yield. Morpeth, forwarding Hawtrey's letter to Phipps, wrote on 5 November: 'The hostility of Coleridge appears to me quite implacable, and his vehement nature will probably carry Dr. Hawtrey with him. The real College authorities (that is the Provost and Fellows) are pledged to support the Great Western.

'The others (the masters) have great opportunities for canvassing among old Eton connections, and they get them to come forward with rigmarole stories about old bathing places – Lord Denham for example last Session. But how far this would prevail in another Session of Parliament is beyond the reach of prophesy'. Phipps also went to see Hawtrey, but achieved nothing.

In February 1848, as the time approached for the Second Reading of the Great Western Bill, a meeting at Eton was 'unanimous in its determination to oppose the projected line of railway, and to follow up its opposition by petitioning both Houses of Parliament'.

When the Bill came up for its second reading on 24 March, Gladstone took the lead in opposing it in the interests of Eton. The *Windsor Express,* which by now had changed its attitude and was prepared to welcome the Great Western branch line into the centre of Windsor as desirable, referred to Gladstone's attack on the bill as 'jesuitical' – not the first nor the last time this epithet was applied to him. The *Express* commented on 'the hackneyed cry of fancied injury to Eton, not having the candour to state that the Provost and Fellows – that is the College proper – lent their warm support to the bill, well knowing that the College and town will and must derive great benefit from the line'. 'Gladstone' continued the *Express* 'was ably answered by Lord Morpeth, who said that he spoke as a minister of the Crown, and with the most lively recollections and warm feelings towards Eton College, when he stated that the Great Western Railway Company had an undoubted right to come to that House and demand powers to construct a line'.

The advantages of a *central* station seem to have become widely accepted. There was acceptance too of the advantages which would ensue from the demolition of George Street, where the station would be situated, whereas a year before the prospect of the destruction of so much property had been deplored. A correspondent of the *Express* referred to George

Street as 'a den of infamy, an abode of filth, of wretchedness and blasting immorality'. The *Express* itself cited one of the great advantages which the Great Western station would bring with it as 'the removal of a wretched neighbourhood'. In the *Express* of 3 June – the day on which the House of Commons Select Committee gave its approval to the Bill – the editor went still further in surveying the anticipated advantages. 'A substantial improvement', he said, 'in the state and condition of the town, as well as its appearance, may now be with confidence looked for. The removal of a great public nuisance, and the substitution for it of a handsome and commodious station, together with sites and facilities for building, a considerable increase in the value of rateable property, the residence in the town of the persons carrying on the business of the railway, and the inducement to reside in Windsor of families connected with London, which the direct communication will afford – are among the advantages on which we may calculate as consequent on the completion of the project now happily so far advanced.'

These sentiments seem completely at variance with those of the previous year. The Windsor Council, however, remained consistent in its opposition to the Great Western. In 1847 it had supported the South Western project to the full and had clearly welcomed the defeat of the Great Western. Now, on 6 April 1848, it adopted a Petition against the new Great Western Bill – though only by nine votes to six. This was, however, the last time the Windsor Council went on record in opposition to the Great Western. Within a year it was negotiating with the Great Western Company for the sale of property needed for the station.

In the meantime the Great Western had gone to the limit in making concessions to win the approval of the College. The curve of the line had been pushed even further to the west away from Eton. 'It does not go into the Brocas field at all', Captain Bulkeley told the parliamentary committee. It provided for all the safeguards the College desired. Batcheldor noted: 'Provost and Fellows approve of present line – altogether out of bounds and does not touch the playing fields of Eton . . . It is the feeling and opinion of the Provost and Fellows of Eton that the proposed Railway will not be injurious to the school or interfere with the boys or their recreation or be inconvenient or dangerous. That every facility will thereby be afforded to the boys in proceeding to their bathing places and no obstructions be offered. That clauses have also been agreed to whereby every facility and protection will be afforded to the scholars and the Provost and Fellows, head and undermaster. That clauses have also been agreed upon in relation to the police regulations during the progress of the works'. The consent of the College was sealed on 17 May and announced to the parliamentary committee on the 23rd.

The Bill was before the Commons Select Committee on six days between 22 May and 2 June, The Provost and Fellows had bowed to what they regarded as inevitable. The masters, however, and many Old Etonians maintained their opposition. Hawtrey and Coleridge re-iterated their arguments. The Old Etonians included Gladstone, Sir Lancelot Shadwell, the last Vice-Chancellor of England (who had not only been educated at Eton himself, but had eight sons who had been at the College and one grandson), and Mr Justice Coleridge. Charles Russell was Chairman, and Charles Saunders, Secretary; I.K. Brunel, Engineer, spoke for the Great Western. It was an imposing array. At the conclusion the Committee announced its approval of the Bill, with its safeguarding clauses. These were far-reaching and perhaps unprecedented. The Provost or his representative was given authority to visit stations and find out if Eton boys were using them. The Company was to provide for the privacy of the College bathing place at Cuckoo Weir. It was to construct the bridge over the Thames as required by the College 'for the purpose of avoiding inconvenience to the scholars of the said school when boating on the said river'. It was to construct bridges as the College required for scholars or floods. It was to keep police officers stationed to prevent Etonians gaining access to the line. No intermediate station was to be constructed without the consent of the College and – with the omission of 1835 in mind – the Company were not to *take up or set down* any passenger, goods or luggage, at any place on the said line between the Windsor Terminus and the Slough Junction of the said line,without the consent in writing of the Provost and College of Eton under their Common Seal'. The College was not going to be caught napping a second time! 'It is all as right as you can wish', commented Batcheldor in a note to the Provost.

At long last it seemed that the Great Western had finally won its long fight. The remaining stages of the Bill would surely be formalities. When, however, the Bill came before the House of

Commons for its third reading in June, Eton discovered that it had another champion — and a very formidable one at that — in the person of Benjamin Disraeli. Disraeli had just become an MP for the county of Buckinghamshire, so that the masters of Eton College were among his constituents. Only two years before Disraeli had established a unique position in the House of Commons as a result of the series of speeches, witty, sarcastic, flamboyant, eloquent, which he had directed against Sir Robert Peel during the debates on the repeal of the Corn Laws. No politician in British parliamentary history had seized an opportunity so unscrupulously or so brilliantly. His presentation of the Tory case against the Repeal made him, almost overnight, one of the party's leaders. For a time he served his nominal leader, Lord George Bentinck, with fidelity, even though Bentinck was basically more interested in the turf than in politics. But in September 1848 Bentinck died and Disraeli became Tory leader in the House of Commons.

This moment had not quite arrived when Disraeli moved his negativing amendment on the third reading of the Bill. The College authorities may have surrendered. But there were 'the Eton masters and the Eton men', both in and out of Parliament, who were prepared to die in the last ditch. Disraeli was prepared to lead the ditchers against the hedgers. The situation had all those dramatic elements which appealed to his romantic imagination and he made the most of it. A few years before he had stayed at the College with the Rev. W.G. Cookesley. During this time he had been engaged in writing *Coningsby,* with its highly coloured account of life at Eton. Disraeli was not an Etonian, but he would undoubtedly have liked to have been one. He could not rectify that, but at least as a parliamentary representative for Eton he could act as its spokesman in the Commons — and what better opportunity than this?

So Disraeli rose to move, as an amendment, that the Bill be read a third time that day six months — the normal Commons procedure for opposing a bill at this stage.

'He stood there', he said, 'as the advocate of his constituents, the masters of Eton School, whose interests were deeply implicated and whose interests, it would be borne in mind, were essentially public interests.' Eton masters had no personal interest, they were not shareholders, they had no private property which would be affected by the railway. 'The masters . . . arrived at the conclusion that the proposed railway would, if constructed, produce irreparable injury to the interests of Eton, to the discipline of the institution, and to the safety of the boys.' He then surveyed the events of the previous year in which the South Western Bill was passed and the Great Western Bill was rejected. The Great Western Company now had the 'hardihood' to bring in a bill similar to that thrown out last year. On that occasion the Commissioners of Woods and Forests had opposed it, but they now supported it, and consequently it had got through to the Third Reading. Was it because the Great Western had offered £25,000?

Disraeli went on to accuse the Commissioners of a breach of faith. The South Western had paid £60,000 on the understanding that the arrangement was conclusive and final. 'And was it to be tolerated that the House should now be called upon to sanction a *subdolous* arrangement, based upon the violation of a solemn engagement?' 'The minister', said Disraeli, 'had received £60,000 from one company to make a conclusive settlement; and £25,000 from a rival company to disturb that conclusive settlement'. 'If the town and park of Windsor', he went on, 'needed to be improved, let a sum of money be voted for that purpose by the House, but let not the requisite sum be taken out of the pockets of any railway company whatsoever!'

Disraeli referred to the circumstances in which the College authorities 'made a panic-struck agreement with the Great Western Railway Company that they would not further oppose them'. This agreement hamstrung the College — but it was still opposed to the railway. He should certainly offer an uncompromising resistance to the further reading of the Bill. The consent of the Crown to it was directly at variance with the course which the Crown pursued in the previous year, and the non-resistance of the College only proved that the College had not been faithful to its duty, and to the trust committed to its charge.

Much of Disraeli's speech was couched — typically — in the language of hyperbole. Some of his statements were, to say the least, tendentious, and it was typical of the man to go out of his way to use the word *subdolous* — which may be interpreted as 'very near to being intentionally deceitful'. But it was a hard-hitting speech which found its mark. After the amendment had been briefly supported by Col. Reid, faithful as ever to the South Western, Morpeth rose. He could, he said, 'leave to the

Great Western representatives in the House the defence of their case, but he had been inculpated in a charge of bad faith and must reply . . . In that very complicated and intricate affair he had acted with the utmost candour, frankness and fair dealing'.

He 'felt there should be some delicacy in treating of the matter' (because of the Queen), but he 'felt it necessary to mention that, in the high quarter to which he had alluded, there was no wish for any increase of railway accommodation between London and Windsor. These views had been conveyed to the Great Western, and Peel could confirm this because he had been consulted on the occasion. Public opinion in Windsor was strongly in favour of railway communication — also of town improvements. In view of this it was considered that if the railway company promoted the improvements so much desired by making the construction of their line harmonise with the scheme to improve the approaches to Windsor, it would enable the Crown, without imposing fresh burdens upon the people, to effect that improvement, and those who represented the Crown would no longer feel called upon to oppose the construction of the direct line from London.

No understanding was ever made with the South Western that if they consented (and paid £60,000) no other arrangement with another company would be entered into. There was no concealment or breach of faith on his part.

As far as Eton was concerned, Morpeth said he was able to bring forward a statement embodying the approval of the governing body to the Great Western line. He read a letter saying that under pressure the College accepted the Great Western line to the west, as infinitely preferable to one passing to the east, 'with the certainty of having a large station close to the private property of the College, with houses and buildings of every description, which would entirely destroy the privacy of the College and playground and interfere with the discipline of the school, and subject them to annoyance of every description'. The letter continued, 'The Provost and Fellows, as governors of the College, are desirous of expressing their sense of the great consideration that has been paid to their interests by Lord Morpeth, in fixing the station of the South Western Railway last year at a sufficient distance from the college and preventing the extension of the line this year, which would subject them to evils from which no legislative enactment could relieve them'.

The House was impatient and there were cries of 'divide'. Four more speakers, however, took the floor before the division was called — Spencer Walpole, who had been Chairman of the Select Committee; Sir H. Vane, who had been in a similar position in the previous year; W. E. Gladstone and F. Scott, a Director of the South Western, who in saying that 'he did not directly call this [the £85,000 paid by the two companies] a bribe' went far towards admitting that there was not much difference. Bearing in mind the long political rivalry between Gladstone and Disraeli, a rivalry founded as much on clash of personality as on conflict of policy, there is something bizarre in finding them standing shoulder to shoulder in defence of Eton. But their style of speech was completely different. Alongside the rhetoric of Disraeli, the language of Gladstone seemed comparatively drab. However, he probably knew much more about the facts than Disraeli and, in a reference to the 'Brocas clump', asserted that 'the real merits [of the Bill] turned on minute topographical circumstances necessarily unknown to the great majority of the House'.

It is clear that every effort had been made to influence the voting of members. Morpeth referred in his speech to the 'extraordinary statement' circulated to MPs.

At long last the Division was called, with the result that 224 were for the Third Reading and 97 against, with a majority of 127. The Bill then went to the Lords and received an unopposed Second Reading on 4 July. What was to prove the last parliamentary battle took place when the Bill came before the Lords Committee. The sittings of the Committee occupied three full days, 18–20 July, and once more the rival forces were ranged against each other. There were still Petitions against the Bill from Eton and from the South Western.

Captain Thomas Bulkeley, Chairman of the Great Western Railway (Windsor to Slough) Company, emphasised all the advantages which would accrue to Windsor from a line terminating in the town. The omnibuses now left Windsor for Slough thirty minutes before the time of the train, and the railway from Windsor would take five minutes. The proposed station would be adjacent to the Castle and to the inns and would facilitate trade.

Bulkeley was one of those who believed there was positive good to be gained in the demolition of George Street. 'It is', he said, 'in a very delapidated state, the most unhealthy part of

Windsor, and it is one of the conditions of the Woods and Forests in order to improve the sanitary condition of the town that we shall pull down the street and have our Station there'. 'There cannot', he continued in answer to a further question, 'be a worse street in any town of England, I should think.'

He dealt in detail with the negotiations with Eton. Clauses had been inserted in the Bill to safeguard the interests of the College, and the Railway Company was bound by the College not to have a station in Eton, although he went on to say that they were quite prepared to have a station at Eton if the College withdrew its opposition. The proposed line of the railway was further west than in the previous bill, outside the Brocas Hedge.

He also made it clear that money was to be given to the Crown to help finance improvements. He said that in evidence on the last Bill Morpeth had said that he preferred one railway to two, but he had also admitted that 'the Court felt themselves under obligations to the Great Western, in having delayed so long making a line into Windsor'.

The evidence of the tradesmen is particularly interesting on the advantages which were expected to accrue from the 'high level' railway. Charles Snowden, grocer trading in Peascod Street, Alderman, JP, twice Mayor, illustrated the position by explaining how his salt came by rail from Droitwich to Slough, then he had to fetch it by road and pay two tolls before it arrived in Windsor. The construction of the branch line would bring it virtually to his doorstep. John Aldridge, miller of Clewer, got much of his corn from Reading; barge transport was inconvenient and sometimes dangerous, especially in winter. And, since there was as yet no road connection near the river between Windsor and Clewer, even when the corn arrived at the wharf, it had to be brought up Thames Street before it could come down Peascod Street to Clewer. The sharp gradient of Thames Street was obviously in the minds and thoughts of many local business men. Henry Thumwood, former coach master, said, 'there are no four horses in the world that can bring two-thirds of a load up the hill'. 'Nothing', he concluded, 'would save the town but getting a railway right in the centre.' So the evidence continued. Arthur Hughes, butcher, had his meat from Smithfields; John Lawrence, builder, had stone and timber come by rail to Slough and then had to transport it by road to Windsor; William Henry Burge, brewer, got his malt from Reading, Abingdon, Wallingford.

Both Brunel and Charles Saunders gave evidence at length. Saunders went through a detailed examination of previous railway projects, including a reference to the possibility of combining with the South Western to make one line and one station. He quoted the Agreement with the Crown in full — referring to the arrangement to pay the £25,000 and to various pledges relating to the station and other buildings. Brunel introduced his evidence by saying that the Great Western had been anxious to come to Windsor for 'a long period past'. He dealt primarily with the detailed planning of the route, with particular reference to the objections of Eton, even the most trivial ones. Coleridge, for example, had said at the previous enquiry that the viaduct 'would not be high enough for a boy with his hat on; he would have to stoop'. The viaduct, said Brunel, would be a flat viaduct, erected upon columns, not arches, 'a continuous colonnade with large openings between the columns', and its height would be 14ft. The previous plan had shown a bridge with one pier in the middle of the river. Eton had objected to this, because of the danger to the College boating, so the bridge had been re-designed as a single-span bridge. A clause to this effect had been inserted in the Agreement. From the bridge the line would rise by a gradient of 1 in 84 'to get up the Castle hill'. On the northern side of the river the line had been put still further out from Eton; there was a written agreement 'not to touch the Brocas Clump'.

He then dealt with the bathing place at Cuckoo Weir, which had figured prominently in the objections of the College. Screening would be provided, but in fact Cuckoo Weir was 250 yards from the Railway at its nearest point. 'I might observe', commented Brunel, 'without the screen it would be perfectly impossible for any person travelling on the railway to see anybody bathing there'.

Rev. Thomas Carter, on behalf of the Provost and Fellows of the College, repeated what he called 'the hearty concurrence' in the line and implied that at various times from 1836 onward the Fellows had been prepared to give their consent.

Then came the opposition. Coleridge, Hawtrey, Gladstone were as inflexible as ever in their antagonism. What a pity that Disraeli was not produced as well as Gladstone! After his brilliant speech in the previous month, his intervention would have enlivened the proceedings.

Among the recreations of the College, the threats to boating, bathing and hockey had been raised. Coleridge added another, namely cricket. 'I do not suppose', he said, 'any man would like to play cricket to bowl through an arch of 14ft. I do not suppose that they would like to pitch the wickets one on each side of a viaduct 14ft high'. Hawtrey could still see no good in the railway. 'Any line whatever which brings Eton nearer to London is prejudicial to the school'. Asked if he was aware that the Great Western was perfectly willing to provide a Station at Eton if he and the Masters did not object, he replied 'that is one of my chief reasons for objecting to the line'.

The sitting on 20 July opened with the evidence of Robert Stephenson, MP, son of George Stephenson. He said that he had attended at the request of the Eton masters — perhaps they considered that his evidence would carry more weight than that of Disraeli. His rivalry with Brunel was apparent in the way in which he spoke. He was fully in favour of the extension of the South Western line into Windsor and implied that there was no need for the Great Western branch. Moreover, a station in Thames Street would be more concealed from the Castle than Black Potts *or* George Street. One of the suggestions he threw out was that of a line from Langley to Black Potts. Langley was the first station on the line from Slough to Paddington and Stephenson's suggestion had several merits — it would provide the link between the Great Western and the South Western which many thought would be advantageous; it would fit into the 'one station ideal' by eliminating the need for a Great Western line from Slough; and such a line would leave Eton and the College playing fields inviolate. Even Brunel had at various times mentioned the possibility of cross-country branch lines, such as one between Ealing and Staines or Datchet.

Next came Lincoln and Morpeth. Neither had much to say that had not been said before. Obviously the overriding consideration with Morpeth was to obtain the Improvements Bill. For this he was prepared to jettison many of his former objections. He now considered the passing of the Great Western Bill 'an indispensable preliminary' to the Windsor Improvements. He went on to confirm that there was an understanding with the South Western Company that, if both the Great Western Bill and the Windsor Improvement Bill passed, 'the South Western Company shall have permission to come through the Park'. 'I am bound to say', he continued, 'that the Crown has the strongest possible objection to a line crossing the Home

Park into Windsor, unless there is an arrangement which it considers of paramount importance being completed, that the Crown will be prepared to waive any portion of that dissent'.

The Chairman of the Lords Committee, the Duke of Cleveland, then brought the enquiry to a close. He made one of the most common sense comments during the whole course of the protracted proceedings when he said that 'the mere possibility of a cricket ball, at sometime or other, being thrown into the window of a carriage' was not 'a sufficient impediment to an otherwise useful project'. The Committee gave its approval to the Bill, the Third Reading followed on 24 July and the measure finally became law on 14 August. On this occasion Windsor did not wait for the Royal Assent. The success of the Third Reading in the House of Lords was deemed to signify victory and was 'announced to the public of Windsor by the ringing of a merry peal from the bells of the parish church'.

The timber viaduct was replaced in the 1860s by the present brick viaduct. This late nineteenth century view from the Castle shows the famous group of elms known as the 'Brocas clump', the railway viaduct and Clewer Church. (EIM)

ABOVE: 'Eighteenth century men struggling, uncomprehending, against the tides of the nineteenth century.' Dr Joseph Goodall, Provost of Eton 1809-40, and Dr John Keate, headmaster 1809-34. Silhouettes by Aug. Edouart. (ML) BELOW: Dr Edward Hawtrey, headmaster 1834-53. From a drawing taken in school. (ML)

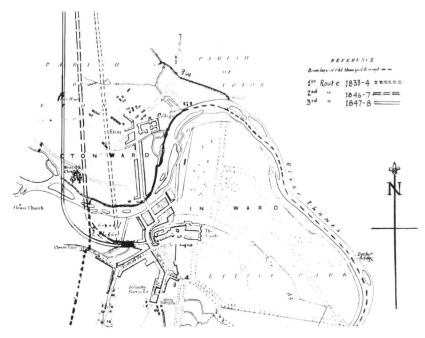

ABOVE: Eton and the Great Western Branch line from Slough to Windsor, showing some of the proposals which eventually put the railway at as great a distance as possible from the College. BELOW: The Great Western Branch line makes its great curve around Eton on its wooden viaduct. Detail of a drawing of the new Eton Parish Church. (GC)

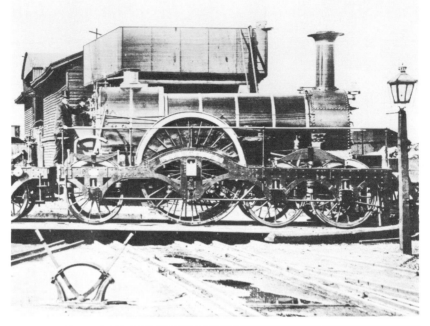

Two of the locomotives which operated on the route between Windsor and Paddington. Both were broad guage locomotives. ABOVE: The Lightning. (BR) BELOW: The Firefly, designed by Jones, Turner and Evans of Newton, Lancs. (BR)

WHO WILL REACH WINDSOR FIRST?

The South Western had got its Act. Now the Great Western had also attained success. Neither, however, had yet achieved its goal. Although it was accepted in the course of 1848 that the South Western would receive the Crown's consent for the extension of its line into Windsor, the necessary legislation had not yet been passed. Nor of course had the final sections of the lines into Windsor been constructed. So, in the story of the rivalry between the South Western and the Great Western, the question still remained, who will reach Windsor first?

During the course of 1848 the construction of the South Western line progressed rapidly. Once the Thames had been crossed at Richmond, the country was flat and there were no engineering difficulties likely to cause delay. Of course the Thames would have to be crossed a second time before the railway could be taken into Windsor, but for the time being the terminus was to be at Black Potts, between half and three-quarters of a mile beyond Datchet, still on the northern bank of the river. The first train travelled from Richmond to Datchet on 22 July to convey the Directors of the Company for the purpose of making an inspection of the bridges and rails. It was hoped that the public opening of the line would take place by 1 August, but, as the result of a subsidence on the Richmond side of Richmond Bridge, this had to wait until Tuesday, the 22nd.

For just over fifteen months — from August 1848 to December 1849 — Black Potts — the station in the field — remained the terminus of the South Western. It was accepted because it was expected to be temporary. None the less it is strange that, after all the fuss that had been made about the hardships and inconvenience of travelling between Windsor and Slough, the Black Potts terminus was regarded as a *Windsor* station. An omnibus service was operated — fares were fixed at 4d per person from Datchet to Windsor and the contractor for

109

the service was Mr. Chater of the Castle Hotel — but the new approach to Windsor across the Home Park was not yet open and the omnibuses had to follow a circuitous route by way of Frogmore to the Park Street entrance to the town. The *Express,* in its first issue after the opening of the line, reported great activity with 'the continual passing and repassing of the omnibuses'. Excursions followed. On Tuesday, 12 September, 'upwards of 400 Wesleyans . . . came in a body per special train'. Another monster arrival took place a week later, again by special train. Each person paid 3s instead of the normal 3s 4d. 700 persons visited the State Apartments and, although the Court was not present, the *Express* feared 'the desecration of palatial privacy, or its conversion into a crowded National Gallery'. Many visitors to Windsor preferred the South Western route to the Great Western and it was reported that the opening of the South Western line had diminished omnibus traffic between Slough and Windsor. An experimental steam-boat service, covering the mile or more of the Thames between Black Potts and Romney Lock, was projected in November. It encountered flood conditions, however, and nothing more seems to have been heard of it.

Soon the advantages of using the railway to shop in London were being publicised. The December issues of the *Express* in the four weeks prior to Christmas carried an advertisement by B. Prew of 'The Great Metropolitan Wardrobe', High Holborn. Under the attractive heading, *RAILWAYS TO LONDON GRATIS,* the public was encouraged to do their Christmas shopping in London and save more than the fare. The inevitable doggerel followed:

'All at Christmas to London a visit who'd pay
Should find out the most economical way . . .
At Prew's you can get; and by purchasing there
Save as much as will pay your up and down fare.'

The terminus at Black Potts could, however, only be a makeshift. As soon as permission was given for the extension of the line over the river and across the Park into Windsor, work immediately went ahead. The *Express* reported that the line would take a sweep of the Park, apparently with a view to keeping the railway as far from the Castle as possible. The definitive Agreement between the Crown and the Company is dated 14 February 1849. By it the South Western had to promise that the Station would be built within two years of the opening of the Railway — 'a handsome and commodious station and all the requisite buildings connected therewith and all works, approaches, matters and things appertaining thereto and all such waiting rooms, sidings or other accommodation for the personal use, privacy and comfort of Her Majesty when using the said railway with such materials in such style of architecture and according to such plans elevations and designs as shall previously be approved of in writing by or on behalf of Her Majesty . . . ' Provision was also made for screening.

After the battles and confrontations of the previous three years what happens now appears an anti-climax. The South Western, Windsor Extension, Bill was introduced into Parliament in February 1849, with Reid and Chaplin as sponsors; it went smoothly through every stage in the Commons and the Lords and received the Royal Assent on 26 June. Of all the Windsor railway bills, it was the only one to go through without a fight. The College secured the insertion of the now familiar 'safeguarding clauses', especially those that related to the prohibition of any intermediate station and to the right of the Provost or his representative to have access to stations.

The interest in fact now shifts to the race to reach Windsor first. If the South Western had had to wait for their Bill to become law, the Great Western must have won. But the decision in August 1848 to proceed immediately with the extension of the line into Windsor was acted upon vigorously and in July 1849 the Company announced that it hoped to open the line for passenger traffic on Monday, 15 August. To achieve this the Company committed the deadly sin of working on Sundays. Eton protested strongly and Horn, Secretary to the South Western, replied saying that the men 'have been given peremptory orders that the practice be not repeated under any circumstances'.

In the meantime the Great Western, although it did have to wait until its Bill became law, did its utmost to make up for loss of time. A few days after the Royal Assent had been given, Saunders wrote to Batcheldor, 'We shall be ready now to commence on works almost immediately to the discomforture, I apprehend, of our very numerous foes'. Construction began in September and at one time the Company was 'working all hands night and day'. Accidents were frequent, an indication perhaps of the pressure exerted on the navvies. On 3 November 1848 while the labourers were at work on the line near Chalvey the sidings suddenly fell in, and completely buried three of the men — one escaped with severe bruises, the other two had broken legs and other injuries. In March 1849 George Norman, aged 17, working by moonlight, caught his arm in the wheel of a truck, as a consequence of which his arm was severely fractured. In September Joseph Cripps, working on demolition in George Street, fell 40 feet — he was injured but not severely. Later in the same month Joseph Moyser, a rivetter employed on the bridge over the Thames, fell backwards into the water while working; his head struck one of the piles; he was rendered unconscious and immediately drowned. This was the price that had to be paid for bringing the railway to Windsor.

Spiritual comfort was, however, made available. A tent — which became known as the Railway Church — was erected in May 1849 in Datchet Lane for divine service for the labourers working on both railways and for their wives and families. Local clergy officiated at the services, but the *Express* reported in June that patronage was limited.

The South Western does not seem to have suffered the accidents that marred the progress of the Great Western. Emphasis seemed to be placed rather on the shortcomings of the service. An increase in fares in January 1849 — 3s 4d to 4s 2d 2nd class return, Datchet to Waterloo; 5s 4d to 6s 8d 1st class return — caused, according to the *Express* 'considerable surprise and no little dissatisfaction and annoyance'. The Editor continued, 'There appears to be little doubt that the whole of the £60,000 in the shape of increased fares, and other charges, will ultimately come out of the pockets of the public who travel by the line between the Waterloo station and Windsor'. There were grievances too about unpunctuality. 'A Daily Passenger' complained to *The Times* that trains had been 30 minutes late in leaving Datchet, 45 minutes late at Waterloo. The *Express* also took exception to the railway companies charging 1d for their time-tables and printed the time-tables itself.

The Great Western line from Slough to Windsor was not by the standards of the time an especially difficult project. But it was a bigger task than the South Western extension. Embankments and cuttings at the Slough end, the timber viaduct over the low-lying land, the bridge over the river, the incline into Windsor, the demolition of George Street — all presented problems. By January 1849 the notices to quit had been sent out in

George Street and by the beginning of April the *Express* was able to report that George Street was 'almost annihilated'. The Bridge was originally planned to be a double span bridge with a pier in midstream. Eton, as we have seen, had raised objections to this as dangerous to the boating and Brunel had accordingly redesigned it as a single span bridge. It was constructed of wrought iron, weighed 450 tons and was reported to be 'perfectly unique in all its contrivances'. Its construction was on the arch and tie principle, the ends of the arch being connected by strong metal ties. The bridge was being assembled in July, but there appeared to be no possible hope of the Great Western being ready before its rival.

There is no question that pressure was put on Locke, the SW Company's Engineer, to hasten. On 15 May 1849 the Directors expressed themselves as anxious to open the line into Windsor in time 'to secure a portion of the summer's traffic'. They asked 'whether time might not be gained by using the temporary bridge, if it be strengthened so as to carry a railway train'. Locke opposed this suggestion and replied guardedly that 'should no unforeseen circumstances arise I am not without hope that the road may be laid across the bridge by the middle of July'. Unfortunately for the South Western 'unforeseen circumstances' did arise. On Sunday, 14 August, only the day before the Government Inspector was going to inspect the line prior to opening, a cast iron girder of one of the bridges at Black Potts snapped in two owing to the sinking of one of the piers. Locke, in reporting this disaster — for such it was for the South Western — said: 'The bridge in question is founded on cast iron cylinders, a plan introduced for the purpose of avoiding the delay consequent on the construction of coffer dams in the river. It is the first time that I have ever used this plan. No defect presented itself until about a week ago when the ballast was put on the bridge and after all the beams, roadway and rails had been laid, and they continued so far as to shew me that in their then state they were untrustworthy'.

The Directors recorded that they 'cannot too strongly express their regret' and continued 'they expect a well devised, substantial, well-built, durable and complete bridge and they impress on Mr. Locke the necessity of having it so constructed on the earliest possible day'. Work on the repair of the bridge accordingly began almost immediately, but the South Western had now irretrievably lost the initiative.

113

The construction of the Great Western Bridge was completed in September. On the 20th, the day after Joseph Moyser had lost his life while working on the bridge, the first engine travelled from Slough, crossed the bridge, and arrived in the new station at 8 o'clock. 'The engine was a newly constructed one, having a tender over the boiler.' Brunel came with it. The *Express,* in its following week's issue, commented that 'the new station, erected as if by magic, in the room of squalid tenements, and opening a smiling scene of the wooded uplands in perspective, bids fair to be an ornamental feature to the town'.

The public opening took place on Monday, 8 October. The first train left Windsor for Slough at 8.5 a.m., the journey taking six minutes. The first train into Windsor had left Paddington at 7.5 and, after a wait at Slough, had reached Windsor at 8.30. In addition to the new line, the Company constructed a diverging branch — the Queen's fork — by which Royal and express trains could run up to Windsor without being detained at the junction at Slough.

So the Great Western had got to Windsor first. Work on the South Western was still proceeding and it was not until 22 November that the line was inspected and final preparations made for the opening. This took place on Saturday, 1 December, the first train leaving Windsor for Waterloo at 8.10. After all the hullabaloo and the ringing of church bells when the South Western got their bill in 1847, it seems strange to find the *Express* reporting, 'Very little excitement has been caused in Windsor by the occurrence, and the directors have exhibited a similar nonchalance, since no official announcement was made of the opening till late on Thursday night'. Moreover, the *Express* voiced its surprise at the makeshift nature of the station buildings and the poor access in Datchet Lane — 'a wretchedly narrow street'.

Be that as it may, with the opening of the Great Western on 8 October and of the South Western on 1 December, the railways had come to Royal Windsor and the long chapter of delay, antagonism and controversy had come to an end. If competition continued between the two companies, it was now over the quality of the service provided.

The hope of royal patronage was never far from the thoughts of those who sought to bring the railways to Windsor. The opposition of the Court to the railways being brought to

Windsor must have seemed frustrating, even perverse to those who could see nothing but good in their progress. The railway companies were prepared to go to almost any lengths to reconcile the Crown to their projects. The Crown could dictate their routes, decide the timing, control the design and location of their stations; the companies would provide royal stations or waiting rooms; they would pledge themselves not to have depots at Windsor where repair work could be carried out. And, as we have seen, the Crown used the needs of the railway companies to extract £85,000 from them.

So the Crown made its bargain and the railways came. In December 1848, when the Court returned from Osborne to Windsor for Christmas, there was apparently no thought of using the newly opened South Western line to Datchet. They travelled by South Western to Basingstoke, changed to the Great Western and continued by way of Reading to Slough. The timing of the opening of the Great Western branch to Windsor on Monday, 8 October, 1849, may not have been entirely unconnected with the expected arrival of the Court from Osborne on Wednesday, the 10th. The red carpet was in readiness. But rumours of cholera in the town caused the royal journey to be postponed and, when the Court came three days later on the Saturday, they travelled by train only as far as Slough and thence by road to the Castle by way of Datchet and Frogmore.

When the Court returned to Osborne on Friday, 23 November, they did for the first time use the Windsor station. A Guard of Honour of the 3rd Battalion of the Grenadier Guards was on duty. Russell, Saunders, Brunel and Gooch — the Big Four of the Great Western — were in attendance. As the train pulled out, with Gooch at the controls, the band struck up the National Anthem. The Court was back in Windsor for Christmas and the royal party this time came all the way to Windsor by way of Basingstoke, Reading and Slough. In the New Year, on Tuesday, 12 February 1850, the departure of the Court was attended by a slight mischance which made a nice story for the *Express*. The royal party arrived at the station, the band of the Grenadier Guards struck up the National Anthem, the spectators uncovered — but there was no train! The *Express* report continued, 'Mr. Saunders, the Secretary, looked confused — his co-officials danced about the platform as if the crimson carpet had been as hot as it looked'. The engine, tender and carriages had in fact taken a run of a few hundred yards out in order to get up steam and, after a short delay, 'the splendid mammoth of the rail came puffing back into the station.'

So in a sense the Great Western had added another laurel to its crown. It had reached Windsor first; it enjoyed royal patronage before the South Western. However, it had always been the claim of the protagonists of the latter that, whereas Paddington was a suburban station, Waterloo was within easy reach of the centre of London. But it was not until March 1850 that the Court first used the South Western line from Windsor on their way to Buckingham Palace.

The 'town improvements', which had played so important a part in the prolonged and complex negotiations between the Railway Companies, the Commissioners and the Corporation now went ahead. The considerable sums of money which exchanged hands meant that the Railway Companies, directly and indirectly, helped to pay for the completion of the widening and improvement of Thames Street and High Street, the construction of new roads from Windsor to Datchet, from Datchet to Old Windsor and from Old Windsor to Windsor, as well as two new bridges — the Victoria Bridge and the Albert Bridge — in place of the old Datchet Bridge which was demolished, and the drainage schemes for both the Castle and for the Town. As part of the general re-development the former roads from Windsor to Frogmore and Old Windsor and from Windsor to Datchet by way of Castle Hill were stopped up.

One interesting sequel was the creation of the Home Park — the Home Park Public as distinct from the Home Park Private. This had been severed from the remainder of the Park by the construction of the new road to Datchet. Permission was given to use a part of this land as the site for the Exhibition of the Royal Agricultural Society of England in 1851; and subsequently Queen Victoria expressed her desire that some portions of the land thus excluded from the Home Park as could be made available for the purpose should be thrown open as a place of recreation for the public. Attempts by Eton College to purchase or lease the land between the railway and the river were resisted. On the other hand, the towpath between the Albert Bridge and the Victoria Bridge, passing through the private section of the Home Park, was effectively closed to the public and has been ever since. In the proposals made in recent years for the establishment of a long-distance walk by the Thames, this stretch is always cited as the most important gap. The solicitor to the Commissioners said at the parliamentary enquiry on the Windsor Extension Railway in 1849 that the Crown was given power under the Improvements Act to 'stop up the towpath against all the world but the Thames Navigation Commissioners'.

The coming of the railways undoubtedly provided a further stimulus to the trade and the growth of Windsor. The expansion of the town gained a new momentum in the fifties. Windsor's growth then as now was restricted to the east and north by the Crown lands and the river, but building continued to the south and to the west. The population of Windsor and Clewer at the time of the census of 1851 was 11,217. By 1861 this had risen by 1,269 and the number of houses by 340.

Tourism too increased and it is perhaps at least of symbolic significance that the opening of the new South Western Station in 1851 in place of the makeshift buildings of 1849 coincided with the opening of the Great Exhibition in Hyde Park – in many respects the apogee of Victorian England. The Victorians became inveterate trippers and sightseers as the railways opened up new worlds to them. Special excursion trains ran from Windsor, both to Waterloo and to Paddington, for the many who went to see the Crystal Palace, the wonder of the age. Windsor was now, thanks to the railways, almost on the doorstep of London and during the summer thousands of visitors took advantage of the new facilities to travel to Windsor to view the Castle, to gape at the paintings, the tapestries, the trappings of royalty which adorned the State Apartments, to marvel at the beauties of St. George's Chapel, to watch the changing of the Guard, perhaps – for the lucky ones – to catch a glimpse of the royal family. Even in 1845 the *Express* had referred to 'so vast a concourse of the curious and pleasure-taking portions of the community'. At that time it was still necessary for most of Windsor's visitors to travel from Paddington and then by crowded omnibus from Slough. Now the railways had come and the terminal stations were in Windsor itself, almost beneath the very walls of the Castle. It was true that from the South Western Station the road had to ascend the hill that climbed past the Curfew Tower to King Henry VIII Gateway and in July 1850 the Company wrote to the Council about the nuisance caused by cabmen in the neighbourhood of the Station. 'Passengers', reported the *Express,* 'were constantly mobbed by the cabmen.'

The opening of the new South Western Station took place on 1st May, 1851. Designed by the architect Sir William Tite in Tudor Gothic style, the Station could now be described as 'elegant and commodious'. 'The waiting rooms', said the *Express*, 'are fitted up most appropriately, the one for first-class passengers being very magnificent, a marble chimney-piece and fitting from the old Royal Station at Farnborough . . . It is not too much to say that when the whole of the works are completed, the Windsor station of the South Western Company will be one of the handsomest and most convenient of the kind in the kingdom'. Every detail of the design of the station buildings had to pass the scrutiny of the Prince. The same was true about the tree screen planted at the expense of the Company to conceal the railway from the Castle — but, the Prince insisted, the trees must not shut out the prospect of Eton. So it is appropriate that the cryptograms V and A and the date 1851 should be patterned in dark bricks on the station walls facing the Datchet Road. And, although they are seldom opened and used nowadays, there are still the fourteen huge double-doors for the use of the cavalry, large enough for the trooper to ride his horse straight through to the waiting truck or wagon. And a few yards beyond the station is the building which once housed the royal waiting room, still crowned by the minaret-like turret from which a watchman could give the signal for the approach of the royal party.

There was more than one abortive local railway project in future years, Windsor to Ascot, Windsor to Maidenhead, but the routes of the Windsor railways are the same now as in 1850. The timber viaducts have been replaced, the Western Station has been re-built, the Black Potts Bridge was replaced later in the century, but the pattern of the railways, fashioned amid so much controversy, remains unchanged.

*ABOVE: The original GW Station at Windsor. The roof
is a typical Brunel all-over roof. (GC) CENTRE: The SW
Station at Windsor about 1855. (GC) BELOW: The SW
Station, 1851 (now Windsor and Eton Riverside), with
some of the 14 doors for the use of cavalry and for
ceremonial occasions. (RES)*

119

ABOVE: SW Station Ticket Office, with the original 'Tudor Gothic' ornamentation. In use from 1851 to 1978. By courtesy of the British Railways Board.
BELOW: SW Station and the Castle.

RAILWAYS TO LONDON GRATIS.

All at Christmas to London a visit who'd pay,
Should find out the most economical way ;
To save further trouble to those who'd do so,
The most economical way we will show.
By Railway from every place great and small,
Our plan brings your fare to just nothing at all ;
Whatever the distance may happen to be,
If you'll do as we tell, you'll come carriage free.
Parliamentary trains by this plan you'll surpass—
Save the whole fare, and come by the first class.
Ere Christmas, of course, it is time to prepare,
And fix upon what Winter Clothing you'd wear :
And all over the world, north, south, east, and west,
PREW's GREAT METROPOLITAN WARDROBE 's the best ;
For Gents and Boys Clothing, so choice the display,
They are the pride of all London, the rage of the day,
Best quality, fashion, fit—and what is still more—
The prices so small as ne'er known before.
Over Coats, which the roughest of weather defy ;
Trowsers, warm and well made, will PREW's wardrobe supply ;
Winter Waistcoats in style with which none can compete,
Sporting Coats, too, with every appointment complete,
At PREW's you can get ; and by purchasing there,
Save as much as will pay both your up and down fare.

EVERYBODY on their ARRIVAL in LONDON VISITS
PREW'S GREAT METROPOLITAN WARDROBE,
which is universally admitted to contain the cheapest, choicest,
largest, and most fashionable Stock of Gentlemen's and Youths'
Winter Clothing in the world. The immense saving effected by purchasing at this establishment is found far to exceed the most san-
guine expectations of the strictest economist ; and tends considerably,
if not entirely, to defray the expences generally attached to a visit to
the metropolis, as no other house in the kingdom can possibly produce such first-rate Clothing at such astounding low prices.

☞ Particular attention is directed to PREW's superb Winter
Over-Coats, Paletots, and Wrappers, all of the very best quality,
style, and workmanship, and impervious to the roughest weather.
Riding, Driving, and Sporting Coats, with all the newest improvements. Winter Waistcoats of every description. Trowsers of the
warmest, most elegant, and serviceable materials. Gamekeepers,
Suits, Liveries, &c.

B. PREW,
Tailor, Hatter, General Clothier, &c.,
THE GREAT METROPOLITAN WARDROBE,
295, HIGH HOLBORN,
FIFTEEN DOORS WEST OF CHANCERY LANE ;
CITY BRANCH—36 & 37, ALDGATE HIGH STREET.

*Advertisement retailing the advantages of using the
railways to shop in London, December 1848 (WE).*

121

GREAT WESTERN RAILWAY TIME TABLE.

On and after December 1st, 1849.

UP TRAINS

Daily Trains

From	Mail 1 & 2 a.m.	1st & 2nd a.m.	1st & 2nd a.m.	1st & 2nd a.m.	Mail 1 & 2 p.m.	1st & 2nd p.m.	1st & 2nd p.m.	1st & 2nd p.m.	1st & 2nd p.m.	1st, 2d & 3rd p.m.	1st & 2nd p.m.	1st & 2nd p.m.
WINDSOR	·	8 5	9 15	10 40	12 20	·	2 15	3 0	4 15	5 20	7 25	9 20
SLOUGH	3 35	8 15	9 25	10 50	12 30	1 25	2 22	3 10	4 25	5 32	7 32	9 30
Langley Marish	·	·	9 33	11 2	·	1 37	·	·	·	5 41	·	·
West Drayton	3 47	8 28	9 42	11 11	·	1 46	·	3 22	·	5 52	7 47	9 40
Southall	·	8 38	9 52	11 16	·	1 51	·	3 31	·	6 8	7 55	9 50
Hanwell	·	8 43	9 58	11 21	·	1 56	·	3 36	·	6 15	8 5	9 55
Ealing	·	8 48	10 3	11 35	·	·	·	3 41	·	6 22	8 15	9 59
PADDINGTON	4 15	9 5	10 20	·	1 10	2 15	3 0	4 0	5 0	6 40	·	10 15

Sunday Trains

From	Mail 1 & 2 a.m.	1st & 2nd a.m.	1st & 2nd a.m.	1st, 2d & 3rd p.m.	1st & 2nd p.m.	1st & 2nd p.m.	1st & 2nd p.m.
WINDSOR	·	9 0	·	3 45	6 35	7 35	9 10
SLOUGH	3 35	9 10	12 30	4 0	6 45	7 45	9 25
Langley Marish	·	9 18	·	4 8	·	·	·
West Drayton	3 47	9 27	·	4 18	6 57	7 57	9 35
Southall	·	9 37	·	4 30	7 15	8 5	9 45
Hanwell	·	9 42	·	4 37	7 18	8 15	9 50
Ealing	·	9 48	·	4 43	7 30	8 18	9 54
PADDINGTON	4 15	10 5	1 10	5 0	·	8 30	10 10

DOWN TRAINS

Daily Trains

From	Mail 1 & 2 a.m.	1st & 2nd a.m.	Mail 1 & 2 a.m.	1st & 2nd a.m.	1st & 2nd p.m.	1st & 2nd p.m.	1st & 2nd p.m.	1st & 2nd p.m.	1st, 2d & 3rd p.m.	1st & 2nd p.m.	Mail 1 & 2 p.m.
PADDINGTON	7 45	8 30	10 15	11 0	12 30	1 40	2 45	4 0	5 30	7 0	8 55
Ealing	·	8 41	·	11 11	·	1 51	·	4 13	5 41	7 11	·
Hanwell	·	8 45	·	11 15	·	1 55	·	4 19	5 45	7 16	·
Southall	·	8 50	·	11 20	·	2 0	·	4 24	5 50	7 20	·
West Drayton	·	8 59	·	11 29	·	2 9	·	4 33	5 59	7 30	9 20
Langley Marish	·	9 9	·	·	·	·	·	·	·	7 39	·
SLOUGH	8 15	9 20	10 53	11 45	1 2	2 25	3 18	4 46	6 15	7 50	9 30
WINDSOR	8 30	9 35	11 5	·	1 12	2 40	3 28	4 56	6 25	8 0	9 40

Sunday Trains

From	Mail 1 & 2 a.m.	1st & 2nd a.m.	Mail 1 & 2 a.m.	1st, 2d & 3rd p.m.	1st & 2nd p.m.	1st & 2nd p.m.	Mail 1 & 2 p.m.
PADDINGTON	7 5	9 15	10 15	2 0	5 0	7 0	8 55
Ealing	7 27	9 26	·	·	5 11	7 11	·
Hanwell	7 33	9 30	·	2 14	5 16	7 16	·
Southall	7 39	9 35	·	·	5 22	7 20	·
West Drayton	7 50	9 44	·	2 28	5 32	7 30	9 20
Langley Marish	8 0	9 54	·	·	·	7 39	·
SLOUGH	8 10	10 5	10 53	2 40	5 45	7 50	9 30
WINDSOR	8 20	10 15	11 0	2 50	5 55	8 0	9 40

On Sunday a Train will leave Windsor at 10.40 a.m. to meet the Down Day Mail; and at 2.30 p.m. to meet the 2.0 Down Train. An Omnibus will run from Windsor to Slough, Daily, to meet the 1.25 Up Train, and the 11.45 Down Train; and on Sunday the 12.30 Up Train.

SOUTH WESTERN RAILWAY TIME TABLE.
ON AND AFTER DECEMBER 1ST, 1849.

SUNDAY TRAINS.

Up Trains.

	1, 2, 3 p.m.	1 & 2 p.m.	1 & 2 p.m.	1 & 2 p.m.	1 & 2 a.m.	1, 2, 3 a.m.
WINDSOR	8 25	6 55	4 5	4 10	1 55	8 10
Datchet	8 30	7 1	5 14	4 15	2 0	8 15
Wraysbury	8 37	7 7	5 19	.. 22	2 7	8 22
Staines	8 44	7 14	5 26	4 36	2 14	8 34
Ashford	8 49	7 19	5 34	4 41	2 19	8 41
Feltham	8 56	7 26	5 40	4 49	2 26	8 48
Twickenham	9 4	7 34	5 44	4 54	2 34	8 55
Richmond	9 10	7 44	5 49	4 59	2 40	8 59
Mortlake	9 14	7 55	5 55	5 5	2 44	9 4
Barnes	9 19	7 59	5 59	5 5	2 55	9 10
Putney	9 25	8 8	6 10	5 10	2 59	9 14
Wandsworth	9 29	8 10	6 16	5 16	3 10	9 25
Vauxhall	9 40	8 20	6 20	5 20	3 20	9 35
WATERLOO	9 50					

Down Trains.

	1 & 2 p.m.	1, 2, 3 p.m.	1 & 2 p.m.	1 & 2 p.m.	1 & 2 a.m.	1, 2, 3 a.m.
WATERLOO	9 7	6 30	4 30	4 30	10 7	8 45
Vauxhall	9 15	6 37	4 37	4 37	10 15	8 52
Wandsworth	9 22	6 45	4 45	4 45	10 21	9 0
Putney	9 27	6 51	4 51	4 51	10 27	9 12
Barnes	9 33	6 57	4 57	4 57	10 33	9 18
Mortlake	9 40	9 3	5 3	5 3	10 40	9 25
Richmond	9 45	9 10	5 10	5 15	10 45	9 30
Twickenham	9 54	9 15	5 15	5 24	10 54	9 39
Feltham	10 1	9 24	5 24	5 31	11 6	9 46
Ashford	10 6	9 31	5 31	5 36	11 13	9 51
Staines	10 13	9 36	5 36	5 43	11 20	9 58
Wraysbury	10 20	9 50	5 50	5 50	11 25	10 5
Datchet		9 55	5 55	5 55		10 10
WINDSOR	10 25					

DAILY TRAINS.

Up Trains.

	1, 2, 3 p.m.	1 & 2 p.m.	1 & 2 p.m.	1 & 2 p.m.	1 & 2 a.m.	1 & 2 a.m.	1, 2, 3 a.m.
WINDSOR	8 25		4 25	2 25	12 5	10 30	8 10
Datchet	8 30	7 12	4 30	2 30	12 12	10 30	8 15
Wraysbury	8 37		4 37	.. 37	12 19	10 37	8 29
Staines	8 44	.. 27	4 44		12 24	10 49	8 34
Ashford	8 49	7 32	4 49	.. 49		10 57	8 41
Feltham	8 56		4 56	2 57	12 35	11 2	8 48
Twickenham	9 4		5 4	2 ..	12 40		8 55
Richmond	9 10		5 10				8 59
Mortlake	9 15	5 18	3 15	12 51		9 10
Barnes	9 22	5 24	3 25		9 14
Putney		5 28		1 5	9 25
Wandsworth	9 40	5 38	1 15	9 35
Vauxhall	7 50	5 45	11 20
WATERLOO			

Down Trains.

	1 & 2 p.m.	1, 2, 3 p.m.	1 & 2 p.m.	1 & 2 p.m.	1 & 2 p.m.	1 & 2 a.m.	1, 2, 3 a.m.
WATERLOO	8 15	7 0	5 35	4 35	2 7	12 30	7 45
Vauxhall	8 22	7 15			2 17	12 37	7 52
Wandsworth	8 30	7 27					8 0
Putney	8 36	7 33	5 50	4 47	2 26	10 37	8 6
Barnes	8 42	7 40					8 12
Mortlake	8 48	7 45	6 0	4 57	2 36	12 55	8 18
Richmond	9 0	7 54	6 5	5 2	2 41	12 9	8 25
Twickenham		8 6	6 14			1 9	8 30
Feltham	9 14	8 13	6 21			1 16	8 39
Ashford		8 20	6 26	5 15	2 54	1 21	8 46
Staines	9 25	8 25	6 33	5 25	3 5	1 28	8 51
Wraysbury			6 40	5 30	3 5	1 35	8 58
Datchet			6 45		3 10	1 40	9 5
WINDSOR	9 30						9 10

OPPOSITE AND ABOVE: Two of the earliest timetables for the trains between Windsor and London. BELOW: Windsor's two-fold railway communication with London – the Great Western to Paddington and the South Western to Waterloo.

REDUCED FARES. DAILY EXCURSIONS.
FROM WATERLOO AND VAUXHALL BRIDGE STATIONS.

Covered Excursion carriages are attached to the following trains.

TO WINDSOR,

On Week days, from Waterloo Bridge, at 9.45 A.M. and 10.50 A.M.   Returning from Windsor at 6.15 and 8.30 P.M.

On Sundays, from Waterloo Bridge, at 9.30 A.M.   Returning from Windsor at 8.25. P.M.

Fares there and Back, 2s. 6d.

These tickets are available at Waterloo Bridge, Vauxhall, or Windsor, but NOT at intermediate Stations.

TO RICHMOND AND TWICKENHAM.

On Week Days.	From Waterloo	Returning by the Trains leaving	
		Twickenham	Richmond
	9. 5 A.M.	4. 5 P.M.	4.10 P.M.
	10. 5 „	„ 6.20 „	„ 6.25 „
	11.15 „	„ 7.30 „	„ 7.35 „
	12.15 P.M.	„ 8.25 „	„ 8.30 „

Fares there and Back, 1s.

TO HAMPTON COURT.

On Week Days, from Waterloo Bridge, at 9.0 A.M., 10.30 A.M., 11.45 A.M., and 2.0 P.M.   Returning from Hampton Court at 7.15 P.M. and 8.50 P.M. daily.

Fares there and Back, 1s.

Tickets are also issued for these Carriages at the Vauxhall Station. These Excursion Tickets are only available at Richmond, Twickenham, Hampton Court, Vauxhall, and Waterloo Bridge Stations.

To KEW and Back, by all trains, 1s.

VIRGINIA WATER.

On Week Days, from Waterloo Bridge, at 10.50 A.M. and 1.50 P.M.   Returning at 4.50 P.M. and 8.30 P.M.   On Sundays, at 9.45 A.M.   Returning at 8 P.M.

Fares there and Back,—First Class, 4s.; Second Class, 3s.

Children under Three Years, Free ; Three to Twelve Years, Half-fares.

CHEAP EXCURSION TRAINS
TO
ISLE OF WIGHT,
PORTSMOUTH, WINCHESTER, SOUTHAMPTON, and to FARN-BOROUGH (for ALDERSHOT CAMP), and back the same day,
EVERY SUNDAY,

From WATERLOO BRIDGE and VAUXHALL STATIONS for PORTS MOUTH at 7.45 A.M., returning at 7.0 P.M.; and for FARNBOROUGH, WIN-CHESTER, and SOUTHAMPTON at 8.0 A.M., returning from SOUTHAMPTON at 7.30 P.M., WINCHESTER at 8.0, and FARNBOROUGH about 9.15 P.M.

Fares.

To PORTSMOUTH, SOUTHAMPTON, or WINCHESTER, and BACK,

First Class, 9s.; Closed Carriages, 6s. 6d.; Covered Carriages, 3s. 6d.

To FARNBOROUGH (for ALDERSHOT CAMP) and BACK,

First Class, 5s.; Closed Carriages, 4s.; Covered Carriages, 3s.

Railway Excursion Poster 1857.

THE SEQUENCE OF EVENTS

1824-25	First projects for railway between London and Bristol
1830	Liverpool and Manchester Railway
1833 (Jan)	Great Western Railway Company formed. Branch line to Windsor first proposed, then dropped.
(Sept-Dec)	London and Windsor Railway Co. formed in opposition to Great Western
1834 (March)	GW Bill receives Second Reading in HC London and Windsor Railway project dropped
(June)	GW Bill passes HC, but defeated in HL
(Sept)	Second GW Bill
1835 (Aug)	GW Bill becomes law, with safeguards for Eton and no branch line to Windsor
1838 (June)	GW line opened from Paddington to Taplow
1839	Abortive negotiations for a 'Windsor and Slough' line
1840 (June)	Slough Station opened
1841 (June)	GW line open from London to Bristol
1844 (Oct)	Windsor Junction Railway Co. formed
1845 (Aug)	Project finally abandoned through opposition of Crown
(Sept)	Formation of Windsor, Slough and Staines Atmospheric Railway Co.
1846 (Feb)	Bill introduced into Parliament
(May)	Bill rejected by HC Committee
(July)	Change of Government. Morpeth becomes Chief Crown Commissioner
(Oct)	Windsor, Staines and South Western Railway Co. formed, Both SW and GW meet Crown Commissioners
(Nov)	Agreements between Railway Companies and Crown
(Dec)	Railway meeting at Guildhall
1847	SW, GW and Windsor Castle and Town Approaches Bills go into Parliament
(May)	HC Committee support SW Bill but reject GW Bill. Town Appraoches Bill deferred

(June)	SW Bill becomes law
(Oct)	Further meetings between Railway Companies and Crown
(Nov)	New Agreements between Railway Companies and Crown
1848 (March)	GW Bill receives Second Reading in HC
(June)	GW Bill approved by HC Committee, opposed unsuccessfully on Third Reading and passed by HC
(July)	GW Bill passes HL
(Aug)	GW Bill becomes law
	SW line opened to Black Potts
	Crown approval to SW to extend line into Windsor
1849 (June)	SW Windsor Extension Bill passed
(Aug)	Collapse of Black Potts Bridge
(Sept)	Construction of GW Bridge completed
(Oct 8)	Opening of GW Branch line
(Nov 23)	Court travelled from Windsor by GW for first time
(Dec 1)	Opening of SW line to Windsor
1850 (March)	Court travelled from Windsor by SW for first time
1851 (May)	Opening of the new SW Station

BELOW: View of the South Western Railway and the Castle. The print shows an early South Western train traversing the gantry which was subsequently replaced by an earthen embankment. (GC)

REFERENCES

Page	Line	
13	20	See 'History of the Great Western Railway', Vol One, by E.T. MacDermot, Revised ed, 1964, p 2.
14	23	WE 7 Sept 1833
	30	WE 16 Nov 1833
	39	BCRO Maidenhead Corporation Minutes 31 Dec 1833
15	7	*ibid* 2 June 1834
	13	WE 23 Nov 1833
	18	WE 11 and 18 Jan 1834
	34	WE 28 Sept 1833; 12 Oct 1833 et seq; 23 Nov 1833
	41	WE 28 Sept 1833 and 23 Nov 1833
16	9	WE 23 Nov 1833
	20	BC 22 Feb 1834
	25	WE 23 Aug 1845
	28	WE 28 Sept 1833
	37	HB p 33
	39	WE 11 and 18 Jan 1834
17	17	WE 18 Jan 1834
	23	A copy of the Report is in ECR
18	1	For full text of the Petition see HB pp 36-6
	19	BC 1 Feb 1834
	32	See BC 18 Oct 1834 for a full account of the Bristol meeting
19	12	WE 8 Aug 1846
	26	HB p 48
	28	HB p 35
	33	BCRO Maidenhead Corporation Minutes 25 Feb 1835
20	6	HLRO HL Select Cte. Minutes of Evidence, G.W. Rly Bill 11 Aug 1835
21	42	ECR 'Eton College Case'
	38	ECR Batcheldor to Duke of Newcastle 10 Aug 1835
23	4	ECR 24 Aug 1835
	13	BC 29 July 1835
	22	G.W.R. Act 1835. Sections 99–103
24	1	ECR 7 Apr 1838
	12	ECR Saunders to Bonsey 20 Apr 1838 (copy)
	23	ECR Judgment of Vice-Chancellor on Eton's application for an injunction, 2 June 1838
	39	ECR G.W.R. Co to College 9 July 1838
25	3	ECR Batcheldor to G.W. 12 July 1838
	9	ECR W. Sims to Batcheldor 6 Aug 1838
26	7	HLRO HL Select Cte. Minutes of Evidence, Windsor, Staines and S.W. Rly Bill 7 June 1847
	11	ECR 27 Dec 1839
33	16	HLRO HC Select Cte, Minutes of Evidence, Windsor, Slough and Staines Atmospheric Rly Bill 8 May 1846

	28	*ibid* 13 May 1846
34	11	*ibid* 13 May 1846
	16	*ibid* 5 May 1846
	26	*ibid* 5 May 1846
	34	*ibid* 14 May 1846
36	22	WE 28 Feb 1846
37	1	WE 19 July 1845
	32	WE 29 March 1845
37	42	WE 19 Oct 1844
38	19	WE 5 Oct 1844
	22	WE 16 Nov 1844
	25	WE 5 July 1845
	32	*ibid*
39	3	WE 16 Nov 1844
	13	WE 28 June 1845

39 32 Milne to Forbes 16 July 1845. The correspondence between the Cte of the Windsor Junction Rly and the Crown Commissioners is reproduced WE 23 Aug 1845

| 40 | 42 | HLRO HC Select Cte, *op cit* 7 May 1846 |
| 42 | 6 | WE 6 Sept 1845 |

42 13 ECR Samuel Warren (College Counsel) to William Tooke (College Solicitor) 9 May 1846

42 15 WE 24 Jan 1846 ECR College Petition 1846

43 2 ECR E.P. Williams to Batcheldor; nd, probably Feb 1846

43	10	WE 14 Feb 1846
	22	WE 14 March 1846
44	2	HLRO HC Select Cte, *op cit* 8 May 1846
	3	*ibid* 5 May 1846
	7	HB pp 136-7
	37	HLRO HC Select Cte, *op cit* 6 May 1846
45	4	*ibid* 7 May 1846

45 15 *Dublin Evening Mail,* quoted C. Hadfield, Atmospheric Railways, 1967 p 44

46	9	HLRO HC Select Cte, *op cit* 12 May 1846
	15	*ibid* 6 May 1846
	20	*ibid* 6 May 1846
	26	*ibid* 15 May 1846
	38	*ibid* 13 May 1846
47	18	*ibid* 13 May 1846
	29	*ibid* 7 May 1846
	34	*ibid* 15 May 1846
48	16	*ibid* 5 May 1846
48	21	ECR Darvill to Batcheldor 16 May 1846
	32	HLRO HC Select Cte, *op cit* 14 May 1846
49	5	*ibid* 14 May 1846
	12	*ibid* 14 May 1846
50	7	*ibid* 19 May 1846
55	18	WE 18 July 1846
56	15	WE 8 Aug 1846
	26	WE 22 Aug 1846
	39	WE 8 Aug 1846
57	23	WE 5 Sept 1846

58	2	WE 26 Sept 1846
	11	WE 10 Oct 1846
59	4	WE 12 Dec 1846
62	9	WE 13 March 1846
	41	HB pp 145–6
63	30	ECR
	37	ECR The correspondence relating to the contro-versy extends from 9 Jan to 3 April 1847
65	18	RA Windsor PP 53 Morpeth to Phipps 15 May 1847
	31	WE 12 June 1847
	40	PRO RAIL 755.1 Morpeth to Directors of Wind-sor, Staines and S.W. Rly. Letter dated 1 June 1847 recorded in Minutes of Directors 15 June 1847
66	1	*ibid* Minutes 1 June 1847
	6	HLRO HL Select Cte. Minutes of Evidence, Windsor, Staines and S.W. Rly Bill 7 June 1847. Col. Reid's evidence is on pp 1 – 100
67	4	*ibid* James Bedborough's evidence is on pp 119–146
73	12	HLRO HL Select Cte, Minutes of Evidence, Wind-sor, Staines and S.W. Rly Bill 23 May 1848
	17	HLRO HL Select Cte. Minutes of Evidence, G.W. Rly (Windsor to Slough) Bill 20 July 1848
	30	quoted Eliz Longford, *Victoria R.I.,* 1964 p 54
74	18	WE 2 Nov 1844
	25	BC 18 Jan 1834
	32	RA Windsor PP p 55. Phipps to Morpeth, nd, about 31 Oct 1847
75	5	HLRO HC Select Cte. Minutes of Evidence, Wind-sor Staines and S.W. Rly Bill 19 May 1848
	11	RA Windsor M20/53 Royal Household and Civil List 1841-4
	28	*ibid* M20/54
	36	*ibid* PP p 55
76	3	HLRO HC Select Cte. Minutes of Evidence, G.W. Bill 23 May 1848
77	28	Dict.Nat.Biog
	32	Harriet Martineau, *Biographical Sketches,* 4th ed, 1876 p 142
	42	RA Windsor PP p 57 Saunders to Phipps 22 May 1848
78	3	*ibid* PP p 57 Phipps to Saunders 24 May 1848
	25	*ibid* C23/75 Peel to the Queen 15 Feb 1846
79	40	*ibid* PP A5 Morpeth to Anson 5 Nov 1846
80	9	ECR Drake to Morpeth 20 Jan 1847
	23	RA Windsor PP p 53 Morpeth to Phipps 15 May 1847
	29	*ibid* Morpeth to Phipps 18 May 1847
81	1	HB pp 148–9
	11	RA Windsor PP p 55 Morpeth to Phipps 29 Oct 1847
	18	*ibid* PP p 56 Phipps to Morpeth 8 Nov 1847

	22	*ibid* PP p 55 Morpeth to Phipps 29 Oct 1847
	32	HLRO HL Select Cte. Minutes of Evidence, G.W. Rly (Windsor to Slough) Bill 20 July 1848
82	3	*ibid* 18 July 1848 Charles Saunders' evidence on the Agreement with the Crown is on pp 154-228
82	9	*The History of the King's Works,* Vol VI. J.M. Crook and M.H. Port 1973 p 393
	37	HLRO HL Select Cte. Minutes of Evidence, G.W Rly Bill 20 July 1848
	40	*ibid*
83	1	*ibid*
	22	RA Windsor PP p 185
84	33	HLRO *op cit* 19 July 1848
	39	ECR Memo of meeting held 28 Apr 1848
85	3	ECR Bethell to Provost 29 March 1848
	10	ECR Morpeth to Saunders 23 May 1848
	19	HLRO HC Select Cte. Minutes of Evidence, Windsor, Staines and S.W. (Slough Extension and Deviations) Bill 2 June 1848
	30	HLRO HL Select Cte. Minutes of Evidence, G.W. Rly Bill 20 July 1848
	31	ECR Morpeth to Saunders 23 May 1848
	35	PRO RAIL 755.1. Minutes of Directors, Windsor, Staines and S.W. Rly 26 Aug 1848
89	10	Lytton Strachey, *Eminent Victorians,* Essay on Dr. Arnold
	24	A.D. Coleridge, *Eton in the Forties,* 2nd ed 1898, pp 25, 27
91	9	*ibid* p 370
	14	There is a biographical article by Noel Blakiston on Thomas Batcheldor (with portrait) in the Annual Report of The Friends of St. George's, 1964, pp 177-181
93	28	ECR Saunders to Batcheldor 14 Oct 1846
	33	*ibid* 5 Nov, 20 Nov, 16 Dec, 23 Dec 1846
94	10	RA Windsor PP p 53 Morpeth to Phipps 16 May 1847
	15	*ibid* Morpeth to Phipps 18 May 1847
	24	*ibid* PP p 55 Morpeth to Phipps 29 Oct 1847
	32	*ibid* Phipps to Morpeth nd
	40	*ibid* PP p 56 Hawtrey to Morpeth 30 Oct 1847
95	4	*ibid* Morpeth to Phipps 5 Nov 1847
	17	WE 12 Feb 1848
95	22	WE 25 March 1848
96	1	WE 22 Apr 1848
	24	HB pp 153-5
	34	HLRO HL Select Cte. Minutes of Evidence, G.W. Rly Bill 18 July 1848
	37	ECR May 1848
97	21	Great Western Windsor Branch Act 1848, 11 & 12 Vict., c.cxxxv; clauses xxiv – xxix
	38	ECR Batcheldor to Provost; nd
98	34	WE 24 June 1848 gives a detailed report of the debate

101	28	HLRO HL Select Cte. Minutes of Evidence, G.W. Rly Bill 18–20 July 1848
105	18	WE 22 July 1848
	23	WE 29 July 1848
109	20	WE 5 and 26 Aug 1848
	32	WE 15 July, 16 and 23 Sept 1848 and *passim*
110	18	WE 4 Nov 1848
	24	WE 2 Dec 1848 *et seq*
	38	WE 23 Sept 1848
111	13	The South Western, Windsor Extension, Bill 1849, 12 & 13 Vict., c.xxxiv
	29	ECR Horn to Batcheldor 9 Aug 1849
	36	ECR Saunders to Batcheldor 24 Aug 1848
	39	WE 2 Dec 1848; 17 March 1849; 15 and 22 Sept 1849
112	18	WE 26 May and 16 June 1849
	25	WE 6 and 13 Jan; 10 Feb 1849
113	8	WE 7 July 1849
	17	PRO RAIL 755.1 Minutes of Directors, Windsor, Staines and S.W. Rly 15 and 29 May 1849
	28	*ibid* 29 Aug 1849
114	7	WE 29 Sept 1849
	12	WE 13 Oct 1849
114	27	WE 1 Dec 1849
115	19	WE 13 Oct 1849
	25	WE 24 Nov 1849
	37	WE 16 Feb 1849
116	12	WE 9 March 1849
117	4	HLRO HC Select Cte. Minutes of Evidence, S.W., Windsor Extension, Rly Bill 30 Apr 1849
	30	WE 5 July 1845
	42	WE 6 July 1850
118	5	WE 14 May 1851
	11	RA Windsor PP p 4. The Royal Archives contain a number of letters relating to the design and siting of the station
	17	*ibid* Page to Phipps 6 Nov 1849. See also RA Windsor C 81/115, 117, 119 (Correspondence between Lord Seymour, Office of Woods, and Phipps, 10, 12 and 15 Jan 1851)

Abbreviations:

BC	Berkshire Chronicle	HLRO	House of Lords Record Office
BCRO	Berkshire County Record Office	PRO	Public Record Office
		RA	Royal Archives, Windsor Castle
ECR	Eton College Records		
		WE	Windsor Express
HB	The Fifth Hall Book of the Borough of New Windsor 1828-52 (Windsor Borough Historical Records Publications Vol 3)		

The line given is to the beginning of the reference.

INDEX

132

SUBSCRIBERS

Presentation copies

1 HER MAJESTY THE QUEEN
2 The Royal Borough
3 Lord Charteris of Amisfield GCVO,
   OBE, QSO
4 Windsor Library
5 Eton Library
6 Maidenhead Library
7 Slough Library

8 Raymond and Marjorie South
9 Clive Birth
10 B.D. Plant
11 The Royal Library, Windsor Castle
12-26 Berkshire County Library
27 M.S.G. Curnuck
28-29 Peter Kingswood
30 Victoria and Albert Museum
31 Stephen & Vicki Wegg-Prosser
32 John Walker
33 Malcolm Read
34 David Read
35 Nicola Brooker
36 Peter Chard
37 Margaret & Brian Whitelaw
38 Mrs J. Waltham
39 M.J. Waltham
40 Patrick Purchase
41 Rev. Kenneth Bradford MA
42 Jim Cannon
43 The Durning Trust
44 Dr. N.A. Routledge
45 Candis Roberts
46 Bryan Hooton
47 John Phillips
48 John Cox
49 Gavin Roynon
50 Derek R. Waters
51 D.A. Bruce
52 Philip Skottowe
53 Eton College Library
54 Mrs Pamela Delamere
55 R.P. Snelling
56 P.E. Jones
57 Mrs J. Kirkwood
58 Mrs C.M. Adock
59 Leslie Sutton
60 Rev. P.R.L. Morgan
61 D.W. Money
62 David Curtis
63 Lina & Mike Cole
64 R.H. Koch
65 L.H.G. Nicolson
66 David C. Hedges
67 D.H. & P.G. Shaw
68 Denis J. Downham
69 Edward Whiteley
70 E.J. Singer

71 Tom Middleton
72 D.P. Vaughan
73 A.M. Jervis
74 John B. Dyson
75 Florence Meech
76 Charles Stainer
77 Mrs L.M. McRae
78 A.W. Sampson
79 Miss E. Gould
80 Harold H. Basford
81 R. Maund
82 Harry J. Fenech
83 B.M. Douglas-Hamilton
84 Tim Ackland
85 R.W. Tibble
86 E.K. Rodbard-Brown
87 L.E. Smith
88 Bernard E. Batchelor
89 Maureen & Geoffrey Reynolds
90 C.J. Holliday
91 Mary Letitia Johnson
92 Francis Woodall
93 Joss & Margaret Mullinger
94 G.N. Webb
95 George Leonard Soper
96 Chas. H. Shepherd
97 N.M. Waring
98 Mrs C. Keeler
99 Mrs J.P. Frith
100 Mrs D.M. Clark
101 Clifford Howard
102 Grace Stephen
103 A.R. Titchener ACIS
104 Thomas William Smith
105 Derek Victor Allen
106 D.A. Barnard
107 P.D. Barnard
108 R.N. McRae
109 Brenda Williamson
110 C. Joan Brighty
111 P.J. Begent
112 David R. Nicholls
113 Mr & Mrs K.R. Akery
114 S.W. B. Watson
115 Alan Bowers
116 John Crump
117 G.E. Heape
118 Mr & Mrs Paul J. Ayres
119 T.J. Greenaway
120 Alan F. Hall

121 Mrs Patricia Jones
122 Keith C. Jones
123 David Jeffenson
124 Doris E. Caine
125 Paul Raymond Evans
126 Dr. D.K.M. Thomas
127 Peter Hjul
128 Arthur Wells
129 R.L. Bull
130 William H. Boniface
131 Col. R.O. Mells
132 Edward Harbeed
133 Leslie Grout
134 Mrs Ida Baker
135 Mrs Hilary Brooks
136 Richard Shaw
137 Alwena & Ralph Maddern
138 Sheilah Horder
139 G.B. Warner JP
140 David Sillince
141 P. George
142 Constance Denby
143 Mr & Mrs G.E. Hobbs
144 J. Stradling
145 A.E. & D.E. De'ath
146 J.J. Howorth
147 J.T. Clarke
148 R.L. Simmonds
149 Dr. E.C. Willatts OBE
150 Arthur Wells
151 G.H. Littleton
152 J.C. Hunter
153 John Kinross
154 James Kinross
155 D.J. Poynter
156 Eton College Geography Library
157 Mrs Olive Gosling
158 J.H.M. Weston MA, JP
159 Velimir Ivan Stimac
160 Michael Thomson
161 Timothy Feeney ACA
162 Martin Feeney MA (Cantab)
163 F.J. Alderman
164 Mrs E.A. Emery
165 M.J. Beardsmore
166 Brian Wickham Atkinson
167 John Newman
168 The Earl of Carlisle
169 Gordon Cullingham
170 Judith Hunter
171 Richard Shaw
172 Mrs Ida Baker
173 Rev John Hirst
174 G.S. Parker
175 Stephen Mason
176 M.J. Hay
177 Chris Reeve
178 Mrs Muriel Stillwell
179 R.R. Bolland
180 Barbara Thompson
181 Michael Burstall
182 Brigette Mitchell
183 K. Buckingham
184 C.J. Buckingham

185 S.W. Higgins
186 Doris L. Charlish
187 J. Douglas Perret
188 Bruce Harron
189 Jane Langton
190 Kathleen Shawcross
191
192 Dr H.W. Parris
193 Joe & Ruth Newman
194 David W. Hughes
195 Christopher James Gilson
196 G.J. Fido
197 G.M. Hall
198 A.G. Brown
199 D.C. Williams
200 D.S-F & W.J. Lanehart
201 J.F. Hoppe
202 Mary Stella Graham
203 Frederick Price
204 Lillie F. South
205 J.E. Prickett
206 Mrs E.R. Davies
207
208 Mr & Mrs Clive Moulton
209 Brian Galloway
210 Windsor Girls's School
211 Gordon G. Gullingham
212 Windsor Grammar School
213 Cox Green Comprehensive School
214 Patrick Benham
215 Henry Nelson
216 Robert F. Gummer
217 Mrs C. Buck
218 Olive May Tarrant
219 Alan Gillies
220 Maurice Bond
221 Windsor Girls' School
222 Trevelyan Middle School
223 Rev Denis Shaw
224 E.S. Barnwell
225 Alan A. Jackson
226 F.E. Thomas
227 Ernest A. Day
228 M.A. Brett
229 A.V. Heath
230 D. Cawsey
231 Aubrey D.V. Holmes
232 Giles Clifford
233 John Norbury
234 J.A. Stratton
235 Miss E.M. Pocock
236 G.J. Fenton
237 V. Ann Buckle
238 H.G. Thomas, MInstTA
239 S.D.S. Moody
240 Ronald Edwards
241 David Willmott
242 Roy Stannett
243 Rita Jane Learwood-Griffiths
244 Peral Teagle
245 G.W. Howard
246 A.N. Falder
247 William Yarrow
248 J.R. Petty

249 Janet Chown
250 W.J. Austin
251 Marten Collins
252 Roman Iwaschkin
253 Jane Dowling
254 Brian Edgar
255 Peter F. Gray
256 Roger G. Cullingham
257 G. Mark Cullingham
258 A.C. Kelsey

259 J.W. Scott
260 R.C. Palin
261
262 Mrs S.R. Ballance
263 Mrs Richard Tozer
264 Bryamor & Carole Davies
265 Bedworth County Middle School
Remaining names unlisted

KEY TO CAPTION CREDITS

RM:	Reading Museum & Art Gallery
WE:	Windsor Express
GC:	Guildhall collection
ILN:	Illustrated London News
TC:	Thamesdown Council
NPG:	National Portrait Gallery
ICE:	Institute of Civil Engineers
ML:	Maxwell Lyte's History of England
EIM:	English Illustrated Magazines
RES:	R. E. Shaw
RRH:	R. R. Holmes, Windsor
VM:	Viscount Morpeth.
BR:	British Railways Board

Endpapers: Aerial View, showing the castle, the College, the Western railway line on the left and the Southern beyond the Castle, with Romney Island and the River in the background and the Home Park to the right.